# Holy Rewired: Science, the Gospel and the Journey Towards Wholeness

MISSIONAL PRESS

Visit Missional Press's website at www.missional-press.com

Copyright © 2010 by W. David Phillips

ISBN 10: 0-9825719-1-7
ISBN 13: 978-0-9825719-1-0

All rights reserved. No part of this book may be used or reproduced in any manner whatsoever without written permission, except in the case of brief quotations embodied in critical articles or reviews.

Printed in the United States of America

Scripture quotations marked NLT are taken from the Holy Bible, New Living Translation, copyright 1996, 2004. Used by permission of Tyndale House Publishers, Inc., Carol Stream, Illinois 60188. All rights reserved.

Scripture quotations marked NASB are taken from the New American Standard Bible, © 1960, 1962, 1963, 1968, 1971, 1972, 1973, 1975, 1977 by The Lockerman Foundation. Used by permission.

Scripture taken from The Message. Copyright © 1993, 1994, 1995, 1996, 2000, 2001, 2002. Used by permission of NavPress Publishing Group.

# Holy Rewired: Science, the Gospel, and the Journey Towards Wholeness

**THE PROBLEM** ........................................................................... 1

    THE HEART ................................................................... 4
    GOD'S SOLUTION ........................................................ 5
    THE CHURCH'S REACTION ........................................ 7

**CHANGE IS HARD.** ................................................................. 10

    HOW DO PEOPLE TRY TO CHANGE BEHAVIOR? .......... 13

**WHO YOU HAVE BECOME** ..................................................... 21

    A BIBLICAL EXAMPLE ................................................. 22
    LIFE EXPERIENCES AND SELF-PRESENTATION ......... 32

**BROKEN EMOTIONS** ............................................................... 35

    DEFINING EMOTIONS .................................................. 36
    THE EMOTIONAL PATH ............................................... 38
    THE ROLE OF EMOTIONS IN A PERSON'S LIFE .......... 41

**WIRING THE BRAIN** ................................................................ 50

    HOW THE BRAIN WORKS ............................................ 51
    NEUROPLASTICITY ..................................................... 54
    WIRING AND BEHAVIOR ............................................. 55
    EXPERIENCE AND PLASTICITY .................................. 57
    THOUGHT AND BRAIN PLASTICITY ........................... 58

**THE CHANGE PROCESS** ......................................................... 64

**THE DISCIPLINES AND COMMUNITY** .................................. 67

    PRAYER ........................................................................ 69
    SPIRITUAL READING .................................................. 73

## EMOTIONAL HEALING ........ 76
### DEALING WITH OUR EMOTIONS ........ 79
## REWIRING THE BRAIN ........ 83
### PART OF MY JOURNEY ........ 83
### REWIRING THE CIRCUITS ........ 85
### COUNTERING ........ 86
### ENVIRONMENTAL CONTROL ........ 91
### REWARDS ........ 92
## A COMMUNITY OF EDITORS ........ 94
### SOCIALLY TRANSFORMING NEIGHBORHOODS ........ 95
### A LOOK IN THE MIRROR ........ 96
### THE LOSS OF COMMUNITY ........ 98
### BRINGING IT ALL TOGETHER ........ 103
## BEING YOU ........ 106
### IMAGO DEI ........ 106
### THE SOCIAL CONTEXT OF BIBLICAL IDENTITY ........ 114
### REBIRTH ........ 117
## REWIRING TAKES TIME ........ 122
## NOTES ........ 125

## MANY THANKS

This book is a product of a long journey. Many people have helped me on this journey and I would like to say thanks.

To those who helped edit this book, I want to offer my deepest thanks. I have discovered how bad a writer I am through this. You, however, helped me get better. Thank you Val Gresham! You helped by editing my doctoral dissertation. You were able to understand what I was saying and helped me say it better. You are the best! Thank you Rocky Porch Moore! You offered suggestions on an early draft. Your help was invaluable. Thank you Brenna Phillips for reading this and correcting my grammar.

To those who offered suggestions, I want to say thanks. Thank you Chuck Conniry for all your help on my dissertation and for being such a great reader and mentor. Thank you Duane Wilson for reading it and encouraging me to keep going.

To those who have been a part of my journey, challenging me, encouraging me, and coaching me, I owe you more than I could ever repay. Thank you Todd Littleton, for being such a great friend and sounding board. Your encouragement and wisdom means so much to me. Thank you Fred Antonelli! Your coaching, listening, and friendship have been invaluable.

*Holy Rewired: Science, the Gospel and the Journey towards Wholeness*

I cannot thank you enough for all you have done.

Sam Raynor, thank you so much for all your work on the cover of the book. You have a great gift. Keep using it!

Len Sweet, I want to offer you my deepest gratitude. You demonstrated such grace, humility, and wisdom during my doctoral work. You have blessed me more than I could ever express. Thank you for pouring your life into my life.

To all my colleagues at George Fox's LEC5 cohort, I cannot thank you enough for your investment into my life as we walked together. You challenged me and encouraged me on this journey.

To Mission Fellowship Church, you are the best. You have allowed me the opportunity to learn, and you learned with me. Your support and gratefulness has been a blessing.

To my parents, William E (Buster) and Margaret Phillips, your love, compassion, and provision through these years has been wonderful. I am proud to be your son!

To my wife, Brenna Phillips, I cannot thank you enough for putting up with me and my uniqueness. You have stuck with me through better or worse, sickness and health, and I cannot wait to grow old with you together. God has allowed me to have a wonderful companion on life's journey, and I am so thankful that companion is you!

To God the Father, God the Son, and God the Holy Spirit, I offer you my deepest praise! You can do anything, far more than I could ever imagine or guess or request in my wildest dreams! Thank you for setting my life right, and forming me into the image of Christ.

## THE PROBLEM

In many communities of Christ followers, there is the belief in the innate desire for a relationship with God. It was that way in the beginning. The second chapter of the book of Genesis describes the relationship between the Creator and the created. Man and woman walked in the garden together in complete love and in an unbroken relationship with God.[1] There was intimacy and peace, love and acceptance. Genesis 2 and the relationship of Adam and Eve with God in the Garden is the story of "the fatherly God who is near."[2] It was a place where all their needs were met.[3] They were whole.

When Adam and Eve sinned by choosing to disobey God, that relationship with God was distorted. The *eikon*, the image of God in which humanity was created,[4] was cracked. The perfect reflection of God was now a broken mirror and a separation of their relationship occurred.[5] The image of God was still present, but this distortion resulted in humanity no longer *living* as those made in the image of God,[6] or reflecting his true nature and character. Humanity, once living in perfect happiness and union with God, finds itself helpless, afraid and hiding from God.

What is the result of this? Humanity is helpless. Humanity craves a relationship with God but that relationship is broken.

Yet humans try to fill that relationship with something, anything that brings some inkling of that relationship. Pascal, in his *Pensees* X.148 helps us understand this when he says,

> *What else does this craving, and this helplessness, proclaim but that there was once in man a true happiness, of which all that now remains is the empty print and trace? This he tries in vain to fill with everything around him, seeking in things that are not there the help he cannot find in those that are, though none can help, since this infinite abyss can be filled only with an infinite and immutable object; in other words by God himself.*[7]

Humanity's broken relationship with God results in the brokenness and helplessness of humankind.[8] Consequently, we struggle to do the right things. Instead of doing what is right, we often do the destructive actions we do not want to do. We distort the facts at work, we tear people down with our words and we hurt people with how we express our anger. There always seems to be a struggle to do what we should and not do what we should not do. There are times we just cannot stop ourselves. There is an inner conflict; there is an embedded desire to live right lives but an inability to do so because of the brokenness that results from sin.

Not only do we cause harm to others, but we also live with the impact other people's brokenness has upon us. Through no fault of our own, we often experience the wrath of others. People have their homes and possessions stolen from them because another person "needs" to support his drug habit. A co-worker berates you in the office because her husband beat her last night. A group of people so obsessed by a social or cultural injustice, perceived or real, forces you to give away rights and freedoms so that those disadvantaged can have their fair share. No one is immune from the brokenness humanity has brought upon itself.

Sin, from the Greek *hamartia*, means to miss the mark.[9] In Aristotle's *Poetics*, the word is usually translated "tragic flaw" or "tragic mistake."[10] Richard Rohr, expanding on the idea of "missing the mark," states, "Sins are fixations that prevent the energy of life, God's love, from flowing freely."[11] He views sin as self-erected barriers that cut people off from God and from their own authentic potential. Ron Martoia notes:

> [W]hen we look at human sin, most of it swirls around our efforts to produce Garden [of Eden] type benefits and satisfactions that just can't be duplicated outside that context. We could say that sin is a fundamental effort to experience something the Garden had for us in its original setting, but through brokenness we attempt to experience it in inappropriate ways. When we end up alienated from God and need restoration, we are seeking a return to the Garden that is available only when we are in relationship with the God of the Garden. We are in exile, seeking a return to our homeland.[12]

Sin is humanity trying to be like God. We are attempting to find wholeness, meaning, and life within ourselves rather than looking to and being that perfect reflection of God. Sin is a result of us being at odds with God, competing for control and authority. Yet, we also have that inner longing for a restoration of that garden environment ever since the Fall occurred.[13] That inner yearning puts us at odds with God, and often times even at odds with ourselves.

## The Heart

The sin of the one, namely Adam, introduced sin into the heart of us all. This is termed *original sin*.[14] This sin created a brokenness in us that reveals itself in unhealthy desires, desires that flow from the heart.

In the Old Testament, the most often used word for heart is *leb*, which meant the seat of one's intellectual and spiritual life.[15] It is also the seat of a person's emotional life and is the origination point of the will.[16] Therefore the word heart encompasses multiple, interrelated aspects.[17] It is the person with all of his or her urges. The overarching meaning is that the heart is the totality of the person. It is "a comprehensive term for the personality as a whole, its inner life, its character."[18]

In the New Testament, the word *kardia* is used to refer to the heart. *Kardia* frequently describes the place of intellectual and spiritual life.[19] However, a striking feature of the word is its interconnectedness to the word *nous*, or mind. These two terms can be used in parallel (2 Cor. 3:14ff) or even synonymously, depending on what aspect of the meaning the author is trying to emphasize.[20] "The element of knowledge is more heavily emphasized with *nous* than with *kardia*, where the stress lies more on the emotions and the will. Thus [the heart] is the person, the thinking, feeling, willing, ego of man, with particular regard to his responsibility to God."[21]

The heart, then, is the totality of the person. It includes the emotional, intellectual, and spiritual aspects of a person. Based on this, we could deduce that the injection of sin into the *heart* of humanity has introduced brokenness into the *totality* of humanity. With the mind, will, and emotions of human beings laid bare from the ruinous impact of sin, the now-destructive nature of mankind would lead them to choose to sin, thus producing broken and hurting people who long for wholeness and hope.

Sin introduced brokenness into the emotional, cognitive, and physical aspects of humanity. As fallen beings, humanity, therefore, has an identity crisis. Humanity's relationship with God is broken, and it does not understand who it is.[22] — BECAUSE IT IS BROKEN WE DO NOT UNDERSTAND WHO WE ARE. Emotional brokenness deprives a person of emotional health, which affects how he makes decisions, reacts to experiences, and lives in relationship with others.[23] It also creates unhealthy and destructive behaviors that can wreck relationships as well as the human experience.[24] It can lead a person to damage and destroy his or her body physically through addictions to food, sex, and legal and illegal drugs. These behaviors are an attempt to bring comfort resulting from a lack of emotional health.[25] It — MEDICATE - THE PAIN also damages the person's relationship with God, the One who created humanity for relationship and in whom true identity and wholeness is found.

So what's a God to do?

**God's Solution**

From the foundation of the world, God had a plan in place to see that we could journey back to that wholeness that humanity found in the Garden. Christianity calls this the Gospel. Embracing the gospel—the person and message of Jesus—allows for the journey towards wholeness. If sin has produced brokenness in our lives, the restoration that occurs from embracing the totality of the Gospel would enable a journey towards wholeness, towards the Garden where God met every need, our relationship with God was in perfect order and sin would no longer impact our lives.

Unfortunately, some people today preach an overly simplistic gospel: Jesus died for the sins of humanity, and if we place our faith and trust in Christ, we get to stay out of hell and live in heaven when we die.[26] However, the gospel is bigger than that. It transforms the *whole* life, not just one aspect. The word for salvation in the New Testament, *sodzo*, which is associated with the gospel, is the same word for healing - total physical, emotional and spiritual healing. It other words, wholeness.[27] The Gospel is more about experiencing a sense of God's *shalom* – wholeness and wellness[28] - than escaping the clutches of hell. The gospel also announces a life lived under the reign of God as depicted in Isaiah.[29] Thus, our desire to be God will no longer be necessary because we have situated ourselves underneath the rule and reign of God. He is our King. He is Father. He is our "daddy."

Entrance into this relationship depends upon repentance. Repentance is not simply a call for people to feel sorry about their actions. In the Bible, repentance was a call for "Israel to prepare for the end of her exile as a nation and to change agendas, specifically in the way she was not being the nation that God intended her to be. It was a call to re-engage with God's original purpose for Israel."[30] The nation of Israel had lost its identity, and it was time for the nation to re-orient and re-align its life around God and to be a blessing to the whole world.[31] For individuals, repentance is a call to a person to rediscover his or her identity as being created in the image of God, re-orienting his or her life around God, and beginning the process of restoration through a personal relationship with God and others who have responded to the covenant love of God.

The gospel, therefore, introduces us to *the* transformative relationship, name Jesus. Jesus is the one relationship that enables us to become the people we were created to be. In embracing Christ, we embark on a journey out of brokenness and into wholeness that will only be complete as God works to restore all of creation.[32] The working out of Jesus and his gospel in our lives, then, is a process where God seeks to re-shape and re-form us into our original identity, and to re-fill us with His original purpose of relationship with God.[33] It also is a process where our relationships are Christ-differentiated[34] – where we are not manipulated or controlled by others, but where we live in peace with others out of an understanding of who we are in Christ.

**The Church's Reaction**

The unfortunate aspect in all of is that a large portion of the institutional Church has dismissed the issues of unhealthy behavior as simply sin or a lack of self-discipline. The antidote for dealing with the behavioral dysfunction, according to those who only emphasize this, is a need to do more things that resemble religious activities: pray more, read the Bible more, and spend more time in church.[35] This prescription is limited in addressing the real cause of destructive behavior. In addition, it does not address the impact of a person's destructive behavior upon another person.

That spiritual prescription also does not take into account the greater complexities of our physical, emotional and cognitive makeup. For example, it does not take into consideration the way in which our minds are created or wired. We have multiple memory storage areas.[36] The emotional memory holds traumatic experiences, which cause a person to react out of pain when he senses he is in a similar situation.[37]

These experiences, while part of the cognitive memory but often forgotten, are rarely readily accessible.[38] These memories must be probed, remembered, and released. When we do this, we are allowed to experience the emotions and feelings associated with emotional memories so that more of the emotions and feelings can be understood.[39] We are then able to accept them as being part of life. As a result, the experience is "re-owned." Once we acknowledge and re-experience the pain of those emotions, hope develops and change can take place.[40] *why?*

Changing behavior, therefore, is not simply a matter of being more disciplined or doing more religious activities such as reading the Bible and praying more. It first requires us to engage the deepest parts of our emotional life because it is by accessing our emotions that we change our behavior.[41] Emotional health allows us to change our thinking about our actions, our relationship to others, and to ourselves. It offers the freedom to regain a healthy understanding of who we are in Christ and our relationship with God the Father. *How we see ourselves — lies that steal, truths that heal*

Changing behavior also requires us to recover who we are as a person created by the Father.[42] The ultimate impact of sin has been to destroy our sense of identity. We have lost the sense of being created in the image of God and being created for perfect relationship with our Creator. In being broken *eikons*, we are searching to discover who and whose we are. Unhealthy behavior is an expression of that searching and longing that is within all people. However, with the restoration of the Potter as we embrace the Gospel, the broken pot can be re-formed into the perfect pot.

So let us take a journey into the heart of the issues with which we struggle. Join me to discover how we can re-discover

## The Problem

who we were created to be, and how we can live holy free - a changed person in how we behave, relate, live life, and reflect our Holy God.

## CHANGE IS HARD.

We all want to change some kind of behavior that we exhibit. Many of us have a little too much weight somewhere that comes from too much food and not enough exercise. Others of us get angry over the smallest items, lashing out at family members, friends or co-workers and making relationships difficult. Still others of us struggle with spending too much money such that our debt load is excessively high.

Major change in inevitable and we will have to deal with it at some point. A friend of mine had a heart attack a few years ago. He was used to eating anything he wanted. He was, from the outside, a model of health. However, he had a blockage that required doctors to insert a stint into one of his arteries. He had to change the way he ate. More chicken, less beef. More vegetables, less butter. He has made the change, thankfully, and is living a normal life. Yet this is not as common as we might think

Most people find it difficult to change. Sadly, most *think* they could do it if they *had* to. A 2007 article in Fast Company magazine however, challenges that thought. The author, Alan Deutschman, states,

Change or Die. What if you were given that

*Change is Hard*

choice? For real. What if it weren't just the hyperbolic rhetoric that conflates corporate performance with life and death? Not the overblown exhortations of a rabid boss, or a slick motivational speaker, or a self-dramatizing CEO. We're talking actual life or death now. Your own life or death. What if a well-informed, trusted authority figure said you had to make difficult and enduring changes in the way you think and act? If you didn't, your time would end soon -- a lot sooner than it had to. Could you change when change really mattered? When it mattered most?

Yes, you say?

Try again.

Yes?

You're probably deluding yourself.

You wouldn't change.

Don't believe it? You want odds? Here are the odds, the scientifically studied odds: nine to one. That's nine to one against you. How do you like those odds?[1]

In November, 2006, at IBM's "Global Innovation Outlook" conference the company's top executives invited the most farsighted thinkers from around the world to come together in New York and propose solutions to some very large problems. They started with the crisis in health care. A dream team of experts took the stage. You might have expected them to tell the group that breathtaking advances in science and technology held the key. That is not what they said. They said that the root cause of the health crisis hasn't changed for decades, and the medical establishment still couldn't figure out what to do about it.[2]

Dr. Raphael "Ray" Levey, founder of the Global Medical Forum told the audience, "A relatively small percentage of the population consumes the vast majority of the health-care budget for diseases that are very well known and, by and large, behavioral." People are sick because of how they choose to live their lives. Levey continued: "Even as far back as when I was in medical school many articles demonstrated that 80% of the health-care budget was consumed by five behavioral issues." While Levey did not bother to name them, most of us could guess what he was talking about: too much smoking, drinking, eating, and stress, and not enough exercise.[3]

The greatest impact upon the conference attendees came from Dr. Edward Miller, the dean of the medical school and CEO of the hospital at Johns Hopkins University. In the discussion on health care, he focused the issue onto patients whose heart disease is so severe that they undergo bypass surgery. About 600,000 people have bypasses every year in the United States, and 1.3 million heart patients have angioplasties -- all at a total cost of around $30 billion. The procedures temporarily relieve chest pains but rarely prevent heart attacks or prolong lives. In about half the cases, the bypass grafts clog up in a few years. About half the angioplasties clog up in a few months. The causes of this restenosis, or the reoccurrence of stenosis which is a narrowing of a blood vessel leading to restricted blood flow, are complex. In some cases, it is simply a reaction to the trauma of the surgery itself. However, many patients could avoid the return of pain and the need to repeat the surgery simply by switching to healthier lifestyles. Very few patients do this. "If you look at people after coronary-artery bypass grafting two years later, 90% of them have not changed their lifestyle," Miller said. "And that's been studied over and over and over again. And so we're missing some link in there. Even though they know they have a very bad disease and they know they should change their lifestyle, for whatever reason, they can't."[4]

Read that again if you are unclear about the consequences. Faced with the choice to change behavior or die, ninety percent of the people choose *not* to change behavior.

## How Do People Try to Change Behavior?

How would you try to change your behavior? Let's look at some ways people try to accomplish this and judge their effectiveness.

### *Willpower*

When people begin to explore behavioral change, one method they try is to simply invoke willpower. People try to break old habits and behaviors and implement new ones on their own without help or a realistic plan. However, whether it is a sin or simply a behavior that needs adjusting, willpower alone will never succeed in dealing with these issues.[5] It may produce outward success for a time, but eventually there will come a time when "the 'careless word' will slip out to reveal the true condition of the heart."[6] In attempting to change behavior in this manner, they are starting with the behavior yet have little understanding as to the cause of the behavior.[7] This is not to say, however, that willpower is unimportant in changing behavior, just ineffective alone.

## Spiritual Disciplines

Christians sometimes seek to change behavior through the implementation of spiritual disciplines. The spiritual disciplines are "those personal and corporate disciplines that promote spiritual growth. They are the habits of devotion and experiential Christianity that have been practiced by the people of God since biblical times."[8] Richard Foster states that the spiritual disciplines are "an inward and spiritual reality"[9] that seeks to bring transformation from the inside. "The needed change within us is God's work, not ours. The demand is for an inside job, and only God can work from the inside."[10]

There are several lists of spiritual disciplines. Richard Foster stresses that there are inward disciplines (meditation, prayer, fasting and study), outward disciplines (simplicity, solitude, submission, and service) as well as corporate disciplines (confession, worship, guidance, and celebration). Donald Whitney's book, *Spiritual Disciplines for the Christian Life* include a list that adds evangelism and journaling, while combining and renaming several in Foster's list. These Disciplines, when followed, foster an experiential relationship with the true change agent, namely the Triune God.

The danger, Foster states, is, "[i]n our enthusiasm to practice the Disciplines, we may fail to practice discipline. The life that is pleasing to God is not a series of religious duties. We have only one thing to do, namely to experience a life of relationship and intimacy with God."[11] The warning Foster issues is a warning not to make the actions primary, but for the person to focus on the relationship with God and others, including how that person works and relates to others. Anything done simply to complete the task does not develop the intimacy and relationship with our Father or others.

However, the Disciplines are not enough to bring total behavioral transformation. Practicing the disciplines often ends up causing people to dwell on the pathology of the issues (the symptoms) rather than working on emotional health and strength. This is actually a form of displacement, protecting people from the more difficult task of behavioral change.[12] Yet, while the Disciplines are not the total path to changing behavior, they do provide a part of the path. Disciplines provide a spiritual framework that opens the door for God's healing, hope, and grace to bring transformation to a person's life. The Disciplines are part of a path that will help "reconstruct [Christ-followers] in the image of Jesus Christ."[13]

### *Accountability/Support Groups*

Another solution to behavioral change that has become popular, at least in American culture and evangelical churches, is the use of accountability groups. These groups include Alcoholics Anonymous, Narcotics Anonymous, Gamblers Anonymous, and other similar organizations.

Research into the effectiveness of twelve step and other support groups shows mixed results. In a 1967 study, researchers looked at the effectiveness of treatment when judges randomly sentenced chronic drunk offenders to one or another of three treatment conditions: a psychiatrically oriented community alcohol treatment clinic, Alcoholics Anonymous, and no treatment. Their research showed no statistically significant differences between the three groups in recidivism rate, in number of subsequent re-arrests, or in time elapsed prior to re-arrest.[14] A study published in 1991 looked at a randomized trial of treatment options for alcohol-abusing workers. In this study, researchers "compared the effectiveness of mandatory in-hospital treatment with that of required attendance at the meetings of a self-help group and a choice of treatment options."[15] Researchers found that "[a]ll three groups improved, and no significant differences were found among the groups in job-related outcome variables."[16] On seven measures of drinking and drug use, however, the researchers "found significant differences at several follow-up assessments. The hospital group fared best and the one assigned to AA, the least well; those allowed to choose a program had intermediate outcomes."[17] Additional inpatient treatment was required significantly more often by the AA group (63 percent) and the choice group (38 percent) than by subjects assigned to initial treatment in the hospital (23 percent). In addition, "[t]he differences among the groups were especially pronounced for workers who had used cocaine within six months before study entry. The estimated costs of inpatient treatment for the AA and choice groups averaged only 10 percent less than the costs for the hospital group because of their higher rates of additional treatment."[18] Other studies have determined that AA attendance can actually lead to poorer outcomes than other therapies.[19] One of the main reasons for this is the issue of adherence to the twelve steps and attendance.[20]

However, other studies show different results. A recent study looked at the impact of religiosity and participation in support groups for addiction. A national survey of groups for addiction was conducted to "identify key differences between participants in recovery groups."[21] The data indicates that "active involvement in support groups significantly improves one's chances of remaining clean and sober, regardless of the group in which one participates."[22] In addition, study participants whose individual beliefs more closely matched those of their primary support groups showed greater levels of group participation. This resulted in better outcomes as measured by increased number of days clean and sober. The study found that religious participants were more likely to participate in 12-step groups. Nonreligious respondents were significantly less likely to participate in 12-step groups. [23]

Additionally, a 2001 study was done with 1,774 low-income, substance-dependent men who had been enrolled in inpatient substance abuse treatment programs at ten Department of Veteran Affairs medical centers around the United States. Five of the programs were based on twelve-step principles, but run by professional therapists. The other five used cognitive-behavioral therapy. The results showed that "[o]ver 45% of the men in twelve-step programs were abstinent one year after discharge, compared to 36% of those treated by cognitive-behavioral therapy."[24] The study concluded that "AA participation preceded reduced drinking."[25]

### *Professional Counseling*

Professional counseling has been effective in dealing with negative, destructive, and addictive behaviors. In a recent position paper by the American Counseling Association's Office of Public Policy and Legislation, the National Institute of Mental Health has shown that "the success rates of treatment for disorders such as depression (70-80%) and panic disorder (70-90%) surpass success rates for other medical conditions."[26] Treatment for heart disease, as an example, has a success rate of 45-50%.[27]

In addition, a 2002 study evaluated the "effectiveness of generic counseling in a primary healthcare setting during three months of counseling and followed up the patients' progress after counseling had finished for the next twenty-one months."[28] In the study, questionnaires were completed by patients within the Dorset Primary Care counseling service. "A naturally occurring waiting-list group was compared with patients receiving counseling at baseline and three months. Measurements were taken of patients' psychiatric symptomatology, quality of life (QOL) and self-esteem."[29] The study showed that patients who received counseling made highly significant improvements compared with those on the waiting list. These improvements were maintained throughout the long-term follow-up.[30] This would indicate, "generic counseling has positive effects that can be maintained for a long period of time after counseling has been completed."[31]

However, other studies specifically in regards to areas of substance abuse, show that mental health professionals often have not fared well in treating this addictive behavior. "Khantzian argued that the proliferation of self-help groups such as Alcoholics Anonymous (AA) occurred because professional responses to substance abuse problems were ineffective."[32] The reason for this was that "professionals were faced with a confusing array of professional and self-help models for substance abuse problems, none of which had demonstrated superior effectiveness."[33]

Having spent several years with a pastoral coach who is a Christian counselor, I can attest to the effect of counseling, particularly Christian-based counseling. However, counseling alone was effective on a limited scale.

What has been effective in my case, and what appears to be effective for others at a point in crisis, is a holistic approach of counseling and information as well as exploring emotional and spiritual areas of life.[34] One method alone does not appear to be sufficient. What one needs is a holistic solution. The science backs this statement up. Let me finish with this story from Alan Deutschman's article "Change or Die."

While the best minds at Johns Hopkins and the Global Medical Forum might not know how to get people with heart problems to their behavior, someone does. Dr. Dean Ornish, is a professor of medicine at the University of California at San Francisco and founder of the Preventative Medicine Research Institute, in Sausalito, California. Ornish, helps us see the importance of going beyond information. "Providing health information is important but not always sufficient," he says. "We also need to bring in the psychological, emotional, and spiritual dimensions that are so often ignored." Dr. Ornish published studies in leading peer-reviewed scientific journals, showing that his holistic program can actually reverse heart disease without surgery or drugs. However, the medical establishment remained skeptical that people could maintain the lifestyle changes. So in 1993, Ornish persuaded Mutual of Omaha to pay for a study. Researchers took 333 patients with severely clogged arteries. They helped them quit smoking and go on Ornish's diet. The patients also attended twice-weekly group support sessions led by a psychologist and took instruction in meditation, relaxation, yoga, and aerobic exercise. Though the program lasted only a year, after three years, the researchers found that 77% of the patients had maintained their lifestyle changes. By doing so, they safely avoided the bypass or angioplasty surgeries that they were eligible for under their insurance coverage. Not only that, but the insurance company, Mutual of Omaha, saved around $30,000 per patient.[35]

*Holy Rewired: Science, the Gospel and the Journey towards Wholeness*

Dr. Ornish developed a holistic solution. Those that he worked with, faced with the choice to live or die, lived. Instead of only 10% changing their behavior, 77% did. This is the process we will explore on our journey towards wholeness.

## WHO YOU HAVE BECOME

You can change your behavior. That is the promise of the scriptures and the re-creative plan God desires. First, however, you have to understand why you act the way you act and how you have come to think and feel the way you do.

Socialization might be a negative word to you but it is a valid word to describe how you become…well, you. It is also a part of what makes up your identity.

Each of us has an identity. Our identity develops from our environment, our family, our social networks, our experiences and even how we think of ourselves. In addition, part of our identity is divine, in that we are created in the image of God, according to Genesis 1:26-27. Though sin distorted that image, it nonetheless still exists within us. Understanding who we have become requires that we examine how our lives have been impacted by our environment, family, relationships, and our relationship with the Triune God. Doing so allows us to see how we view the world, how we act and react in situations, and how we view ourselves.

Our identity is formed in our childhood and is wired in our brains. Thankfully, that wiring is not permanent; it changes as we have different experiences and as we think and behave differently. The brain can potentially change its structure with each different activity it performs, modifying and perfecting its circuits so that it can be efficient in its working. Interestingly, if part of the brain fails, other parts can and will take over those tasks. The name scientists give this brain property is neuroplasticity.¹

The systems and structures that display the greatest plasticity are those most subject to experience and environment.² Every brain system is shaped by a person's experience. Neuropsychologist Chris Frith notes, "[o]ur brain is hard-wired during the first few months of life as a result of our visual experiences."³ The experiences we have and the environments in which we grow up result in a formation of behaviors that, to be changed, must be unlearned by changing the way the brain functions.

All of us have learned behaviors from our childhood. The foundation of how we act, behave and think is our environment. For many of us, the primary relationships in our environment is our family. Peter Scazzero, the author of *The Emotionally Healthy Church*, says that "[o]ur family is the most powerful influential group that has affected who we are today." ⁴ The environments in which we grow up and the environments in which we live provide experiences that are engrained within us. This is how Paul can make the bold statement that bad company corrupts good character.⁵ You become like those you hang around. Much of who you are results from the experiences, actions and thoughts you have with your family, friends and other relationships.

**A Biblical Example**

An examination of the narratives of Scripture can provide evidence to corroborate this. One family tree that we have available to us is the lineage of Abraham found in Genesis 12-37. We are provided, by the author of Genesis, a broad look at many of the actions and experiences of Abraham's children, grandchildren, and great-grandchildren. By observing the actions of Abraham's descendents, we can see how family dynamics and life experiences impact our own behavior. This will give us insight to be able to confirm much of what we already know: we act, think and talk like those with whom we are in deep relationship.

**Genesis 12**. In Genesis 12, God introduces us to Abram, who would be more well-known later as Abraham. Beginning in verse ten, we find the story of Abram and his family traveling to Egypt during a famine. Abram feared that the Egyptian Pharaoh would impose upon his wife Sarah to become one of his concubines. Because of this insecurity, before entering Egypt, Abram told Sarah to tell the Egyptians that she was Abram's sister. He believed that in doing so, the Pharaoh would treat him kindly and spare his life.

When they reached Egypt, Sarah did as requested. As expected, Pharaoh took Sarah to be part of his concubine. He also gave Abram many gifts. However, God sent plagues upon the Pharaoh for the deceit of Abram and revealed to Pharaoh Abram's secret. This led to Pharaoh banishing Abram, Sarah, and all their possessions from Egypt.

We now begin to see some of Abram's character flaws. This is more than sin. His life is filled with deceit resulting from fear. His fear has caused him to want to deceive others for self-preservation and advancement. He did this despite the fact that in doing so he placed his wife in the position of what would be considered adultery in a post-Exodus Israel.

Positively, we also note Abram's propensity for obedience.

In Chapter 12, God approaches Abram with a promise to make him the father of a nation and one who would bless the nations. When God issued a call to follow Him into a land he did not know, Abram embraced the journey without question. He packed his belongings, gathered his flocks, his wife, and his extended family, and joined God on the journey.

**Genesis 15**. In Genesis 15, we are reminded that Sarah and Abram had no children. As Abram considered the idea that God would make him the father of a nation, he wondered to God how this would happen. He had a female servant in his home who was young and could provide him a child. Unless God worked a miracle, Abram saw no way that he himself would be the father of a nation God was building. God spoke to Abram, telling him that a servant would not be the father of the nation. It would indeed be Abram. To demonstrate this, God entered into a covenant with Abram through a covenant ceremony wherein God would bring a child to Abram and Sarah.

**Genesis 16**. God's promise to Abram was a child. Sarah, however, decided that the conception was not happening soon enough. She did not believe God's promise—that despite her age God would bring about a child *through her*. Sarah therefore gave her Egyptian servant, Hagar, to Abram so she could bear a child for him. This was appropriate according to custom, but disobedient according to the message from God and his covenant with Abram. Abram would have a son, whom he, Sarah, and her servant would raise. It would be Abram's son and would allow the fulfillment of promise, at least in Sarah's understanding. Sarah, however, would not be the one to conceive and give birth to the baby. By doing this, Sarah was attempting to circumvent the process and promise of God.

*Who You Have Become*

Upon learning that she was pregnant, Hagar started treating Sarah with contempt, ridiculing her and looking down upon her. Sarah confronted Abram about this. Abram told Sarah that because Hagar was *her* servant, she was to treat Hagar as she saw fit. Whatever Sarah wanted to do to Hagar, *she* needed to do it. As a result, Sarah treated Hagar so badly that Hagar eventually ran away. However, after an encounter with "the angel of the Lord," Hagar returned to Abram. Eventually Ishmael, the child conceived through this relationship, was born to Hagar.

We can note two things from this part of the Abrahamic family. First, Sarah displays a great deal of insecurity, most likely stemming from the pain she feels resulting from Hagar's boasting and ridicule. Sarah was jealous of Hagar. As a result, she makes life unbearable for Hagar. It becomes so difficult that Hagar leaves knowing it might be the end of her and her baby's life. This would show up again in the story of Jacob and Esau and the brothers of Joseph.

Secondly, we see the attempt to circumvent the promise of God. Despite God's assurance that Abram and Sarah would conceive a baby, the plan to bring that promise to reality through what could be considered surreptitious means was executed. Rebecca would do the same thing later.

**Genesis 21**. In Genesis 21, Sarah gives birth to Isaac after eventually getting pregnant herself per God's promise. After giving birth to Isaac, she hears Hagar and Ishmael making fun of Isaac and orders Abram to banish them from the home. Abram is upset because Ishmael is also his son. The Lord, however, tells Abram to do what Sarah said because Isaac is the lineage through which his future descendants will come. The blessing of the nations will come through Isaac.

However, God will also make a nation out of Ishmael because he was also Abram's son. Assured by this, Abram put together food and water for Hagar and Ishmael and sent them out on their own.

Sarah continues to reveal her envy and jealousy. It is so much a part of her that she is willing to risk the death of Hagar and Ishmael just to be rid of them. Instead of working through the issues, the easy way to be relieved of the taunting from Hagar and Ishmael is to have them removed from the community.

Regarding Abram's behavior, however, we can see a continued propensity to be obedient to God. Assured by God's protection, Abram did what God told him to do in putting Hagar and Ishmael out of his hope despite the love he had for Ishmael as his son.

**Genesis 25**. At this point in the Abrahamic story, Sarah has died and Abram marries another wife, Keturah. Keturah gives birth to Zimran, Jokshan, Medan, Midian, Ishbak and Shuah. Yet despite the fact he had more children, Abram gave everything he owned to Isaac. Before he died, he also gave gifts to the sons of his concubine. However, he sent them to a land in the East, far away from Isaac.

In the meantime, Isaac has married a woman named Rebecca. After some time, Rebecca became pregnant with twins. She had a hard time carrying them and went to the Lord asking why they were always struggling with each other in the womb. The Lord said that they were two nations and they would always be at odds. In addition, the older one would serve the younger. When the twins were born, Esau was Isaac's favorite because he, like Isaac himself, was an outdoorsman. Jacob was Rebecca's favorite.

In chapter 25, Abraham plays favorites. He gave everything he had to Isaac, leaving the other sons with nothing. Also, while he eventually did give them gifts before his death, he had them sent away in the pattern of Ishmael. He wanted great distance between Isaac and his brothers.

In addition, there is a pattern of tension between brothers, which leads to one party leaving or being forcibly removed from the household. First, there was Ishmael and Isaac. Isaac and his stepbrothers are then separated. Now, even before birth, God reveals that there will be conflict and tension between Jacob and Esau. In addition, the youngest would rule the oldest, similar to Isaac and Ishmael.

**Genesis 26** Just like Abram, Isaac found himself in the middle of a famine. He had to leave his home and move to Gerar. When the town's men started asking about Rebecca, his wife, he lied and said that Rebecca was his sister. Isaac was afraid that the men would kill him because of Rebecca's beauty. Some time later Abimelech, the King of the Philistines, observed the relationship between Isaac and Rebecca and confronted Isaac. Isaac confessed that he lied because he was worried he would be killed.

At the same time, Isaac hears from God regarding his presence in Gerar. God tells him to stay in Gerar. If he does, God will bless him while he is there. In addition, the promise God made to Abraham will continue on to Isaac. Isaac obeyed, and God blessed him abundantly while he was in Gerar.

Abraham's character is revealed in Isaac. On one hand, because of the beauty of his wife, and because he fears he would be killed by someone who wanted Rebecca as his own, he instructs Rebecca to lie about their relationship. <u>The fear and insecurity of his father continues through Isaac as he is</u>

willing to deceive others, put his wife in danger, and put a nation at risk of guilt for self-preservation. On the other hand, like his father, Isaac obeyed God. When God spoke to Isaac about remaining in the land of Gerar, he did not hesitate. He simply obeyed. God blessed Isaac and his family, brought great prosperity to them as a result of that daily act of obedience.

**Genesis 27.** When Isaac was old and blind, he called to Esau and told him to prepare his father's favorite meal. Isaac did not know how much longer he would live and wanted to bestow the blessing of the first born on Esau. Overhearing this conversation, Rebecca devised a plan that would allow *her* favorite son, Jacob, to receive the blessing. She told Jacob to prepare Isaac's favorite meal and to dress up as Esau. Jacob did as his mother said. He went to Isaac and gave him his meal. Isaac suspected that it was not Esau because of Jacob's voice, but Jacob's wearing clothes with hairy skin on the hands eventually deceived Isaac into thinking that it was Esau. Believing him to be Esau, then, Isaac blessed Jacob. After the blessing, Esau came in and discovered what had happened. Isaac said to Esau, "I have made Jacob your master." From that time on Esau hated Jacob and vowed to kill him. Rebecca, hearing the plans, told Jacob to flee to her brother's home in Haran and she would call for him when his brother calmed down.

The blessing of the firstborn was for Esau, yet Rebecca wanted her favorite son to receive that blessing. She set out to deceive Isaac and in the process benefit Jacob. Favoritism and deceit continue to be lived out in Abraham's family. In addition, Esau expresses the anger and hate found in Sarah. Finally, a brother once again is pushed out of the household. It is important to note that in the bigger theological picture, scripture reminds us of how God used this event to continue His community and nation building through Jacob and not Esau.[6]

**Genesis 34.** Jacob, now named Israel, and his family have arrived in Shechem. One day, Shechem, the prince of the town raped Dinah, the daughter of Jacob and Leah. Soon afterwards, however, the prince fell in love with Dinah and courted her. He and his father Hamor approached Israel to determine if Shechem could make her his wife. In fact, Hamor suggested that Israel and his family intermarry with the locals. Israel, having discovered along with his sons what had happened to Dinah, said they would stay and exchange women only if the town's men were circumcised. The men of the town agreed, due to the size of Israel's fortune and potential for their own abundance. Three days after the "surgery" while the men were still sore, Jacob's sons, Simeon and Levi, entered the town and killed all the town's men including the king and the prince in retaliation for the rape of their sister. Then Jacob's other sons plundered and robbed the town, taking the children and women as slaves. When Jacob heard what had happened, he became outraged. The sons said, "Why should we let them treat our sister like a prostitute?"

When we examine this section of the story of Abraham's family, we notice how the sons of Israel let their anger simmer. When the opportunity arose to exact revenge, they took it. They did not simply take revenge on the perpetrator of their sister's rape, they killed every man in the city and took all the children and women as slaves. They destroyed an entire city because of the hate and anger in their lives. Looking back, we can see these same character flaws in Esau and Sarah. However, as those flaws flowed into the descendants, they become more intense. Sarah simply wanted to put Hagar out. Esau wanted to kill Jacob but did not. Jacob's sons not only wanted to kill those who had harmed their sister, they actually carried out.

**Genesis 37.** Genesis 37 begins the story of Joseph. Joseph's brothers hated him because he was his father's favorite. Also, early in his life, Joseph started having dreams that he was to be ruler over his brothers. When his brothers heard this, they plotted to kill him. Reuben, however, convinced he brothers not to kill him but to dump him in a well and leave him to die. This would be a much better scenario.

Reuben, however, had a plan. The brothers would dump Joseph in a well and leave. He would come back and rescue Joseph and take him back to their father. Before the plan could be executed, however, a group of Ishmaelites came by. Judah, one of the brothers asked, "Why don't we sell Joseph as a slave instead?" The brothers agreed and sold Joseph to the Ishmaelites.

After selling Joseph, the other brothers took Joseph's multi-colored robe and poured goat's blood on it. They sent the torn and bloodied coat to his father with a message: "We found this. Isn't this your sons?" Assuming that an animal killed his son, Israel grieved. Meanwhile, the Ishmaelites sold Joseph as a slave to the Pharaoh in Egypt.

The character issues and the environment created by future generations of Abram can be described in this one story. The brothers of Joseph were jealous of him. That jealousy resulted from the favoritism of his father. In addition, their deceit cost a father time with his son. This deceit can be traced back to Abraham and Isaac, who deceived kings, thinking it would save their own lives. These brothers did not care enough about their own father and the impact it would have on him.

It is important to note at least three common negative patterns through the life of Abraham's family. The first is a pattern of lies and deceit. This is evident in all four of Abraham's generations. A second pattern is that at least one parent in each of the generations has a favorite child. Finally, sibling rivalry and relational cutoff between family members create tension that shows up among the three generations.

We all act like our parents. You actually know this to be true in your own life. I know it is in mine. All of us have that moment in our life when we finally realize that we talk like and act like our parents. I do not specifically remember that moment in my life, but looking back, I can see how I mirrored the behavior of one or both of my parents. One specific behavior that comes to mind is how I used to drink tea at dinner when I was young. My dad used to stick one finger into his glass of tea to keep the ice from coming up to his mouth. When I was young, I would drink tea the same way. I know it is a somewhat simple and silly illustration, but I drank tea that way because it was modeled for me by my father.

I recently sat with a young lady who was telling me that her computer was acting up. Her father, a computer consultant was taking his time getting her computer fixed. She told me a story that I myself live, and that I know well from my father's own behavior. If she were a customer, her computer would already be fixed. Since she was his daughter, though, he was working on it when he had the time; other people come first. I remember that with my own father and how my mother would get frustrated at my dad when there was an issue with one of our cars. Other people would get their cars worked on first. Unfortunately, I mimic that behavior with my family.

John Maxwell has a quote that I remember distinctly because it affected me deeply. Unfortunately, I do not know if it came from a book or something I heard him say at a conference. Regardless, the quote is, "You teach what you know. You reproduce what you are." We need to realize the same habits and hang-ups we ourselves have will most likely be passed on to those in whom we invest our lives, be it our family, co-workers, or friends. They will all take part of you with them.

## Life Experiences and Self-Presentation

A core sense of self develops at a young age, including infancy, from experiences we have in life, including the relationships we have with our family and other caregivers.[7] Intentionally or unintentionally, adults can influence an

> *infant's developing sense of self by selecting and emphasizing certain aspects of the infant's experience. When the child takes a tumble, for example, the parent can reflect back the silliness and fun of the situation, or, conversely, the danger and fear that the child may be feeling, and the child may use this communication to frame his or her own experiences.*[8]

As we get older, we will attempt to control the impressions others have of us. We do this by limiting or controlling the interaction we have with others.[9] We try to control more directly the impressions people form of us. We only let people see what we want them to see. This has been termed self-presentation, which is "the conscious or unconscious attempt to control identity-relevant images before audiences."[10] Through self-presentation, "the person begins with a self-image that he or she believes to be – or wants to be – true of the self and presents that self to some audience. He or she then looks for validation of this identity in the way others respond; the reactions of others provide a confirmation of that identity."[11] This public self-presentation often corresponds with how we perceive ourselves. This is because we often want others to see us in the same way we want to present ourselves, which again, is at least partially shaped from the experiences and relationships we have had in our lives. [12] For instance, if we want others to think of us as the smart one in the room, we may try to gather a lot of information about many topics so we can maintain this perceived identity.

However, we often begin to internalize that public presentation, believing privately what we present in public. In fact, research has shown that a person's self-presenting behaviors often have the greatest impact on the private sense of self when those behaviors are acted out in front of others. A study by Dianne M. Tice asked eighty students to portray themselves in various ways – as introverted, sensitive, and thoughtful or as extroverted, outgoing, and socially skilled – and express that behavior by answering several questions. In this study, half the students performed the behavior in front of an audience. The other half was asked to recite the answers into a recorder alone. After presenting themselves according to their designated behavior and answering the questions, they were asked to rate their true personalities. The results showed that people who self-presented publicly internalized their behavior more than people who did so anonymously. People who were instructed to self-present as introverted started to see themselves as introverts. Likewise, people who self-presented as extroverts began to see themselves in that manner. Conversely, people's ratings of themselves were not affected in the private, anonymous conditions.[13] This study shows that our identity can be shaped by how we present ourselves in front of others. We become what we present to the public. Regardless of whether it is who we really are, it can be who we become.

The environment in which we grow up and the relationships we have, particularly during those early formative years, will affect our understanding about who we are and how we act and feel. It will create our identity. We will behave and think according to that identity. The emotions and behaviors prevalent in that environment will be engrained in our mind. Continuous exposure to people and experiences in that environment will literally wire our brain to automatically produce similar behaviors.

Not only does the environment wire behaviors in the brain, but those experiences can also engrain the same fears, insecurities, and other damaging emotions in us that existed in that environment. Those emotions will drive our behavior, especially destructive behavior, though we may never consciously understand why we behave as we do. If we do not explore the impact our family, other relationships, and other experiences have on our lives, we will recreate that same environment for our own family and close relationships. Those same behaviors and issues can be passed on to others as a result.

There is hope. Our hope comes from being "in Christ." Often, however, before we can experience the hope, we need to confront the impact of our emotions and experiences. That will be the focus of the next chapter.

## BROKEN EMOTIONS

John Kotter is a Harvard Business School Professor and widely regarded as the world's foremost authority on leadership and change. He is the premier voice on how the best organizations actually "do" change. And he has hit on a crucial insight. "Behavior change happens mostly by speaking to people's feelings," he says. "This is true even in organizations that are very focused on analysis and quantitative measurement, even among people who think of themselves as smart in an MBA sense. In highly successful change efforts, people find ways to help others see the problems or solutions in ways that influence emotions, not just thought."[1]

Unfortunately, that kind of thinking is not taught in many business schools, seminars, or leadership courses. In addition, it does not come naturally to the modern leaders who pride themselves on disciplined, analytical, and reasoned thinking. [2]

Contrary to what many of us have been taught for most of our lives, changing our behavior is more than just acquiring more information. It involves renewing our mind. That is clearly what the Bible reminds us in Romans 12:1-2: "And do not be conformed to this world, but be transformed by the renewing of your mind…" Few people, however, really

35

understand the whole process of renewing our minds and rewiring our brains. While we do have to change how we think to see our lives transformed, our thinking begins with our emotions.

For most of my life, I had been under the impression that if I wanted to live differently I needed to learn new information. So I learned and read and studied, hoping that sooner or later I would land on the secret to weight loss, exercise, organization, financial health and other behaviors I exhibited that I just didn't like. I read the books, bought the tapes and attended the seminars. Yet, though I had all the information, it only resulted in short-term changes with long-term disappointments.

Doctoral work with a Christian focus tends to create a Holy discontent. That is what happened for me as I poured through research on behavioral change for three years. It was during this journey that I realized I (and others who had mentored and taught me) had been both wrong and right. Changing behavior does mean changing how we think, the transformation of the mind from Romans 12. However, truly changing how we think requires us to deal emotion's power first.

**Defining Emotions**

Before we go any further, however, we need to define emotion. *Emotion* is a difficult term to define. Even though many people have tried to capture the word's meaning, it is very difficult to arrive at a generally accepted definition. According to Beverly Fehr and James Russell, "Everyone knows what an emotion is, until asked to give a definition."[3] Aristotle and Plato attempted to define emotion, as did philosophers such as Aquinas, Descartes, Hobbes, Hume and Kant.⁴ For the past several centuries, psychologists worked to define emotion, but even with all the research and the scientific and technological advances, a broad, accepted definition has yet to be agreed upon.

Etymologically, the word is composed of two Latin words: *e*, meaning out or outward, and *movere*, meaning movement, action, or gesture. Originally, the word meant moving out of one place and into another.⁵ As the word evolved, it came to mean "a moving, stirring, agitation, perturbation, and was so used in a strictly physical sense."⁶ To be emotional was to be moved, literally, in a physical sense.⁷

Psychologist Daniel Goleman makes this argument. In his popular book, *Emotional Intelligence*, he states that the simple etymology of the word suggests, "that a tendency to act is implicit in every emotion."⁸ He also says, "All emotions are, in essence, impulses to act, the instant plans for handling life that evolution has instilled in us."⁹ Emotions move us to act. They are impulses that push us and cause us to behave.

While not being able to arrive at a clear definition, many psychologists agree that there are three aspects present in emotions. These aspects include:

1. Conscious Experience – emotion can be felt and verbalized;
2. Emotional Behavior – emotional behavior is epitomized in actions such as laughing, crying, and smiling;
3. Physiological Events – these 'events' are primarily the reactions of the nervous system. We begin to sweat when we are afraid, or our heart beats faster when we are getting close to home after a

long absence. These reactions often seem completely out of control.[10]

## The Emotional Path

To better understand the role of emotions in a person's life, it is necessary to understand how the brain functions and how the emotional and rational (or cognitive) work together. Understanding the emotional brain gives us insight into how we were created and what needs to happen to deal with the emotional aspects that help define our behavior. Let's examine the structures in the brain that define how emotions function.

The two main structures in the brain that manage the emotional and rational functions are the amygdala and the neocortex.[11] In humans, the amygdala - from the Greek word for "almond" – is an almond-shaped cluster of structures just above the brainstem. There are two of these structures, one on each side of the brain.[12] The amygdala is the emotional specialist in the brain.[13] If it is separated or disconnected from the other structures in the brain, a person is unable to evaluate the emotional significance of events. Since it holds a person's emotional memory, a disconnected amygdala will result in a life without meaning.[14]

Neuroscientist Joseph LeDoux's research has given us a greater understanding of the information flow between experience, emotion, and cognition. When we receive inputs from our five senses, the input travels first to the thalamus. From there, it branches off on to two separate paths, one to the amygdala and the second to the neocortex. In the first path, information goes to the amygdala and because it is also connected to the neocortex, the input goes through the amygdala into the neocortex. At the same time, the input also travels to the neocortex directly. However, the input reaches the amygdala *first*.

This pathway in the brain is crucial because it saves time in the case of an emergency.[15] However, it carries a limited portion of messages while the major portion of messages takes the longer road to the neocortex. What registers in the amygdala is enough of a signal to issue a warning or other response. Why? In the case of an emergency, a person does not necessarily need to know all the details of the situation to know that he or she is in danger.[16]

Though the amygdala is at work preparing the impulsive reaction, which may or may not be the appropriate response, another part of the brain is trying to prepare a more fitting response.[17] At the other end of a circuit to the neocortex, just behind the forehead, lie the prefrontal lobes.[18] The prefrontal lobes attempt to inhibit the influence of the reactive amygdala. The lobes are at work when someone is afraid or enraged, constraining the emotion to deal more effectively with the environment. This area brings a more thoughtful, analytical response, modulating the emotions.[19]

Goleman states:

> *Ordinarily the prefrontal areas govern our emotional reactions from the start. The largest projection of sensory information from the thalamus, remember, goes not to the amygdala, but to the neocortex and its many centers for taking in and making sense of what is being perceived; that information and our response to it is coordinated by the prefrontal lobes, the seat of planning and organizing actions toward a goal, including emotional ones. In the neocortex a cascading series of circuits registers and analyzes that information, comprehends it, and through the prefrontal*

> lobes, orchestrates a reaction. *If in the process an emotional response is called for, the prefrontal lobes dictate it, working hand-in-hand with the amygdala and other circuits in the emotional brain.*[20]

The key to this happening appears to be the left prefrontal lobe.[21] Neuropsychologists who have done research with people with brain injuries in the prefrontal lobe areas have determined that the task of the left prefrontal lobe is to act as a "damper" or neural thermostat that regulates unpleasant emotions.[22] The right prefrontal lobe is the location of negative feelings, like fear and aggression, whereas the left prefrontal lobe keeps the raw emotions constrained, possibly by inhibiting the right prefrontal lobe.[23]

Without this damper, an emotional hijack can occur. When this happens, "a center in the limbic brain proclaims an emergency, recruiting the rest of the brain to its urgent agenda. The hijacking occurs in an instant, triggering this reaction crucial moments before the neocortex, the thinking brain, has had a chance to glimpse fully what is happening, let alone decide if it is a good idea."[24]

I once had a pastor friend say during a sermon that if someone has kicked your cat, the first thing we must do is to understand that someone has probably kicked their cat. In other words, he was reminding us that hurting people hurt people. When an emotional hijack occurs, someone who is hurting may get upset, even emotionally explode, when an insignificant event happens. The event is simply a trigger that brings out the emotional pain resulting from previous events in that person's life. When people are emotionally unhealthy or environmental factors have created stressful situations, no matter how much the damper of the left neocortex tries to restrict a pure emotional reaction, it may not be able to.

As a result, we feel before we think. As our brain's emotional systems have assessed limited meaning from the situation and are preparing for action, the cognitive, rational systems in our brain are trying to prepare a more educated response. What this indicates "is the likelihood that much of cognition…is merely rationalization to make unconscious emotional response acceptable to the conscious mind."[25] What we determine as rational thought is actually the rationalization of our emotional reaction to the experience we are having.

Wait. Please do not gloss over that last statement. It is powerful. We think we are being rational. We might even think we are being logical. However, all we are really doing is rationalizing our emotional understanding of a situation.

### The Role of Emotions in a Person's Life

Because the brain functions in this way, the emotional brain is key to assigning meaning to any experience.[26] The brain produces an image that integrates past experiences, memory, cultural learning, and other multi-sensory information.[27] Those experiences create an emotional memory that is capable of influencing behavior without a person even realizing emotions are involved. This is because emotional memory is not a "conscious recollection," which is the way the term memory is used in everyday conversation,[28] also called declarative or explicit memory.[29] However, emotional memories, or implicit memories, form from memories of dangerous or threatening situations,[30] and involve implicit or unconscious processes.[31]

An example from the New Testament can help us see how this works. Jesus is moving through the countryside and casting out demons. In an encounter with the religious leaders, they will not give him credit for the work he is clearly doing. They say he is casting out demons not by the power of God but by the power of the prince of demons. This is a truly illogical argument that Jesus exposes. Why do they make that argument? These religious leaders were threatened. Their power over the masses was eroding because of the work of the incarnated God. Jesus was behaving in a way that did not conform to their understanding of the Law. They reasoned that since He did not obey their understanding of the Law and God, Jesus could not be sent from God. The only other option was that the source of his power was from the enemy of God, whom they named Beelzebub. They based their reasoning on their fear, an emotion, not on any logic or reason. To the religious leaders it was quite logical to assume that this man Jesus was not sent from God. They were the keepers of God's truth and they knew better than anyone did, in their own minds, how God would act. This man Jesus was not following those prescribed views; therefore, he must be from the enemy.

In addition, because there is a connection between the amygdala (the feeling area) and the neocortex, (the thinking area) of the brain, emotions are important to how we think. Emotions are important to making wise decisions and allowing us to think clearly.³²

However, emotions have more significance than only making wise decisions. First, emotions organize our lives. Emotions regulate our mental functioning, organizing both our thoughts and actions by establishing goal priorities and then organizing actions.³³ For example, fear motivates us to flee or fight. Anger leads us to prioritize overcoming obstacles and preparing for attack. In addition, emotions set goals that cognition and action work towards, making emotions a critical determiner for conduct.³⁴ Emotions work out the desired goal and cognition provides the best implementation for obtaining that goal. For example, if we were in pain, our emotions would set a goal of being pain free. Our minds then determine the best course of action to become pain free. Emotions, then, are the guiding structures in our lives particularly in our relationships with others.³⁵

Emotions also influence memory and thought, and they exert a great influence on decision-making. They can detract from decision-making, or they can enhance it.³⁶ Emotions enhance decision-making by helping determine how significant particular outcomes are to us. They also help to reduce our options by rapidly and preconsciously appraising things as good or bad for us.³⁷ Left unchecked, emotions become the driving force in how we act because we will act out of our own self-interest.

One of the most important aspects of the brain that helps us understand why the emotions are so important in our behavior is the idea of multiple memory systems, one of which is an emotional memory.

### Emotional Memory

It has been determined that there are multiple memory systems within the brain, each devoted to different functions.³⁸ For example, one memory system allows a person to learn to hit a baseball. Another system causes a person to remember trying to hit a baseball and not succeeding. Still another memory system will make that same person tense when he comes to the plate after having been hit in the head by the pitcher the last time he was at bat. In addition, not only are there different memory systems, but different networks in the brain orchestrate those memory systems.[39]

Dr. Joseph LeDoux tells the story of a French physician named Edouard Claparede. The good French doctor examined a female patient who had brain damage and seemed to have lost the ability to create new cognitive memories. Every time Claparede walked into this patient's room he had to re-introduce himself, even if he left and returned just moments later. One day Dr. Claparede decided to attempt something different. He entered the room as normal and held out his hand to greet the female patient. She reached to shake his hand. When their hands clasped, however, she immediately pulled her hand back. Claparede had hidden a tack in his palm and pricked the patient with it. Interestingly, the next time Claparede entered the room she had no recollection of him but would not shake his hand. She was unable to tell him why she would not shake his hand, only that she would not do it.[40]

Claparede concluded that he had come to signify danger. He was no longer just a man to this woman, but a

> *stimulus with a specific emotional meaning. Although the patient did not have a conscious memory of the situation, subconsciously she learned that shaking Claparede's hand could cause her harm, and her brain used this stored information, this memory, to prevent the unpleasantness from occurring again…the patient's ability to protect herself from a situation of potential danger by refusing to shake his hand reflects a different kind of memory system. This system forms implicit or nondeclarative memories about dangerous or otherwise threatening situations. Memories of this type…are created through the mechanism of fear conditioning – because of its association with the painful*

*pinprick, the sight of Claparede had become a* learned trigger *of defensive behavior (a conditioned fear stimulus).* [41]

Claparede's observation resulted in two important conclusions. The first is that learning is not completely dependent on conscious awareness.[42] In other words, we don't always realize that we are learning something new. Our experiences are teaching us whether we are *aware* that we are learning or retaining anything or not. The other conclusion is that once learning has taken place, the stimulus does not have to be *consciously known* to generate an emotional response. Humans, therefore, have an *implicit* emotional system of memory interdependent from an *explicit* conscious memory. This is the emotional memory.[43]

The impact of both the explicit and implicit memory systems can be illustrated through the description of a car accident. A person is driving down the road and has a terrible accident. In the midst of this accident, the horn is stuck and blares for what seems like an eternity. The person is in pain and is traumatized by the accident. Eventually, the person is rescued and physically the person heals completely. Some time later, the person is riding with a friend and hears the horn of another car. Hearing the horn, the person has physical reactions such as muscle tension and sweating as well as increased blood pressure and heart rate. These are *implicit* bodily responses. The sound of the horn also travels to another memory system, which holds *explicit* memories. When this happens, the person then may be reminded of the facts of the accident. The emotional remembrance occurred through the implicit memory, causing bodily reactions. Without this, the person's conscious memory would be flat, where emotions are numbed, covered and not expressed. The two memories are now unified into a potentially new area of long-term memory.[44]

However, suppose that the accident happened so long ago that the explicit memory system has forgotten details of the event, or even the event itself. If the implicit emotional memory has not forgotten the accident, when a horn sounds, an emotional reaction most likely would be triggered. The person would then have an emotional reaction to the event but not understand why they are reacting to the event. In fact, they may not even realize they are reacting. For this to happen, the emotional memory would have to be less forgetful than the explicit memory system, meaning that it retains memories much longer and with greater detail than our cognitive memory. This appears to be the case.[45]

This is supported by two realities. First, the explicit memory system is incredibly forgetful and inaccurate.[46] The pioneer cognitive psychologist, Ulric Neisser, examined people's memories of the explosion of the Space Shuttle *Challenger* at two different times in people's lives – the day after the explosion and then several years later. While most of the subjects stated that their memories of what they were doing that day were clear, in many instances the memory at the later date was dramatically different than the memory reported the day after the tragedy.[47] Several years after the event, what they were doing had changed. In addition, emotional events are often accompanied by selective amnesia of the experience.[48] This is consistent with Freud's theory that unpleasant events are often repressed. While it is not understood what conditions lead to the loss of memory rather than the facilitation of it, some contend that it relates to the intensity and duration of emotional trauma.[49]

Cognitive memory then has the potential to distort an event if it remembers the event at all. The reason for this is that we have an incredible gift of gist recall, but have a difficult time being exact. Emotional memories do not help completely in the recall, though they do help in some areas of recall. Emotionally arousing material forces your attention on one central focus. However, this makes it difficult to remember all the peripheral details. Therefore, you may remember one part of an event that is emotionally traumatic, but the details surrounding that event may become clouded or distorted over time.[50]

The second reality is that emotional responses tend to diminish very little over time. They actually increase in intensity as time goes on.[51] H. J. Eysenck labeled this the incubation of fear. His proposal attempts to explain the "persistence of neurotic activity and its liability to increase over time."[52] Eysenck argues that under certain conditions, incubation or strengthening of the conditioned response of anxiety will result.[53] When we do react out of our emotional memory, the intensity of the reaction tends to increase over time. Years after an emotionally painful event, our reactions can be worse than right after the event.

Emotion can trigger recollection, and vice versa. The emotion enhances recollection, but at the same time by recollecting those events, you would also remember the emotional response. It could be like a loop in which the emotional systems of the brain interact with the cognitive systems of the brain. This memory loop could help understand the searing recall of traumatic memories in people with post-traumatic stress disorder. Therefore, an emotional event could trigger recall of the event, which would then loop back to a re-experiencing of the emotion of the event. Or, remembering the event may trigger the emotional reaction associated with the event, which in turn could trigger more intense recall, in a continuous loop.[54]

In fact, we may not even realize we are reacting out of that emotion or the extent of the reaction we are having. A wonderful lady I know provides an example of this reaction. Her house is immaculate. She is obsessive about it being clean, that everything matches, and that everything is in its correct location. In her forties, however, this lady is quite controlling. She controls her environment, her childs education and does not like to be told what to do. We were talking about this idea of emotional memory one day as we were talking about the research I was doing in my doctoral work. Later on, she told me that she had thought about what I said and realized events in her childhood may be partly the cause of her controlling behavior. She didn't like milk growing up. However, her mother forced her to drink milk. She had never considered that her disdain for being forced to drink her milk would have resulted in her current behavior, but she was now considering that it might be one of the contributing factors to how she went about her day. In fact, she can sometimes get quite angry any time she feels like she is being forced to do something she doesn't want to do. The emotional memory of that disgust may be the cause her behavior now though she only has begun to realize it.

We can see this emotional impact in the first sin in Genesis 3. When the serpent approached Eve, he first caused her to think about the fruit by asking her a question. Then he appealed to her emotions. As she processed the action, her first response was an emotional response. This emotional response led to thinking, which led to action.

*Broken Emotions*

After both Adam and Eve ate the fruit, their first reaction was an emotional reaction. "I was afraid," Adam said, and out of this emotion, he and Eve created a covering for themselves. Then they hid, also an expression of the fear and shame they felt. That is the pattern: emotion, thought, and then action. To journey towards wholeness, then, we have to bring healing to our emotions.

# WIRING THE BRAIN

Recently, I spent an extended period of time with someone who would constantly make this sucking sound, as if he was sucking out something from between his teeth. Honestly, it was quite irritating. After a while, I had to say something so I asked him why he did that. I also asked him to please stop. He responded that it must have been a habit and he did not realize he was even making that noise. Thankfully, he did stop.

We all do things without realizing that we are doing them. Over the years, behaviors become automatic and not even part of our conscious thought. Some time ago, a similar issue confronted me as well. I was working with a counselor focusing on my eating habits. Part of the process required me to write down everything I ate. I realized after a week or so that when I came home from the office in the afternoon, I would, out of habit, open the fridge and look for a snack, even if I had only recently eaten. That is a habit, I discovered, that was established during elementary school. I would come home from school and look for food. Sometimes the food was snack cakes and other times it was part of the leftovers from last night's meal. I never realized that was happening.

Neurological processes in the brain create habitual

processes that are so automatic a person does not realize how she or he is behaving.[1] In fact, a person's brain is largely under the influence of automatic processes.[2] This is important for a person's survival and productivity. Without these processes, every time a person gets out of a chair to walk to the refrigerator, he would have to decide whether to lead with the left foot or right foot. In addition, people could not drive and talk at the same time. Multitasking would not be possible.[3] We need to understand that the brain is "organized so that once an activity becomes routine it doesn't require conscious effort but occurs automatically."[4] This is by design so we can be active, work hard, and enjoy life.

These habits create patterns of behavior that are wired in the brain. To consider how thinking determines behavior, I want to walk you through how the brain works. This may seem boring and unnecessary. In fact, when I was in seminary, I had to take an introductory counseling class. We learned about all these brain mechanisms. I thought, "This is nuts! What am I going to need to know, as a pastor, what dendrites and neurons are?" I did not really take the class seriously, though I did make a good grade. Now I wish I had taken it seriously. I hope that by helping you see the power of the neural circuit, you can have a completely different perspective on how our thinking determines how we act. I also hope it provides an avenue to understanding how changing our thinking can indeed change our behavior.

**How the Brain Works**

Let us begin with an exploration of how the brain works. The first element of the neurobiological parts of the brain is the *neuron*. The neuron consists of the *soma*, which is a cell body that carries out the major cellular functions.[5] *Dendrites* sprout from the soma. Dendrites are multibranched tentacles that receive incoming messages from other neurons and carry those messages to the soma of the cell of which they are a part. These dendrites are thick at the base but get thinner with each branch.[6]

In addition to the dendrites, a neuron also sprouts *axons*, which are long and fibrous strands that extend away from the soma. The job of the axon is to carry information to another neuron.[7] At the point of connecting to the other neuron, the axon creates tiny storage tanks of neurochemicals called *vesicles*.[8] These storage tanks will release chemicals that transmit messages to the next cell in a created circuit. This is called electrochemical stimulation.[9] At the end of the axon is the *synapse*. The synapse is actually almost nothing. It consists of the axon of the transmitting neuron, the dendrite or the soma of a receiving neuron, and a gap of one-millionth of a centimeter between them.[10] The average brain neuron makes about 1,000 synaptic connections and receives even more of the connections (sometimes as many as 100,000) depending on its function and location in the brain.[11]

When the synapse receives an electrochemical stimulation, it stimulates the movement of calcium ions, which in turn start the process of the vesicles releasing their *neurochemicals* (also called neurotransmitters). These neurotransmitters are the language of brain communication.[12] These transmitters flow through the synapse. This activity will either excite the next neuron or inhibit the firing of the next neuron.[13] If the neurotransmitter creates a positive charge between the receptors in the synapse, the next neuron will create an action potential, a moving pulse of electrical charge that sends information from one neuron to another,[14] causing the next neuron to energize and continue the transmission to the next neuron in the circuit.[15] If a more negative charge is produced, the action potential will be inhibited from occurring and the transmission will stop.[16] Many drugs attempt to enhance or decrease the impact of the neurotransmitters and are used for such things as pain management and Parkinson's disease.

The transmission has a greater potential of producing a positive charge if the synaptic strength, the ease with which a signal traverses the gap between two neurons,[17] between neurons in strong. If the synaptic strength is increased, the possibility of the next neuron energizing is greater. This has led to the maxim, "Cells that fire together, wire together."[18] As one writer stated, "when neurons fire simultaneously, their synaptic connections become stronger, raising the chance that the firing of one will trigger the firing of the other."[19] Synaptic strength is the key to creating neural circuits and to the brain's ability to change. Therefore, it is the key to changing the wiring in the brain, which affects thinking, and thus changing behavior.[20]

Repeated actions, emotions, and experiences wire the brain in such a way that neural connections are strengthened. These connections will create circuits that prime our thoughts and then behaviors. As a result, habits are produced. These habits become automatic and often, unless specifically noted, are not a part of a person's conscious, explicit memories.[21] Changing the wiring that produces habitual behavior requires changing the order of how the brain's neurons fire. The brain's unique ability to do this is called *neuroplasticity*.[22]

## Neuroplasticity

The widely held belief for much of the past four centuries was that the only time the brain changed after childhood was when it began a long process of decline.[23] It was also believed that if brain cells did not develop properly or if they were injured or died, they could not be replaced. Conventional wisdom stated that the brain could not alter its structure or find new ways to function if part of it was damaged.[24] Despite the fact that "[s]tructure and function are really information processing being implemented by the physical and chemical properties made available for biological molecules, cells, networks of cells, and so forth,"[25] it was believed that information processing could not change.

However, in recent years, scientists have made breakthrough discoveries showing that the brain actually changes its structure with each different activity it performs. It modifies and perfects its circuits. In addition, if parts of the brain fail, other parts can and will take over those tasks.

In a study done by Alvaro Pascual-Leon, plasticity caused by environment and experience is demonstrated in a dramatic way. He set out to discover what would happen to adults who suddenly lost their vision.[26] As part of this study, he used volunteers who could see and had normal vision. He then blindfolded them. The volunteers wore their blindfolds all day, every day, from a Monday morning to a Friday evening. They spent their days navigating their rooms in a Boston medical center. They were taught Braille, the system of raised dots representing letters that enables blind people to "read," all the while having their brains scanned while they were engaged in tactile and auditory activities.[27]

Before their five days of "blindness," the volunteers had their brains scanned to create a baseline for observation. The visual cortex of each volunteer showed expected activity: when they looked at something, it was highly active and when they listened to something or touched something, it was inactive. However, during their period of "blindness," scans showed that when the volunteers did tactile or auditory tasks, their visual cortex became active. As the week continued, the brain system responsible for touch became increasingly quiet when the volunteers were feeling the Braille dots. The visual cortex became increasingly active. Neurologically speaking, "the 'seeing' brain was now feeling and hearing."[28] In addition, when the blindfold was removed, the volunteer's visual cortex stopped responding to the tactile and auditory stimuli within twelve to twenty-four hours.[29]

One conclusion of this study suggests that the ability for the visual cortex to feel and hear had always been there.[30] Neural connections that have kept silent (not firing) for decades can be recruited when needed. If those connections were used repeatedly, with the blindfolds staying on for years instead of days, researchers believe that those temporary changes could be made permanent, thus changing the whole structure and mapping of the adult brain.[31]

**Wiring and Behavior**

What does all this mean for behavior? There is an old story used by preachers that demonstrates the impact this has for understanding behavior. A young mother gets ready to cook a ham for dinner. Her daughter, watching and helping her, sees her mother cut off part of the ham before she puts it in the pan. The daughter asks her mother an interesting question,

"Mommy, why did you cut the ham before you put it in the pan?"

The mother responds, "Because my mother did it that way."

"Why did she do it that way?"

"I don't know, dear, but let's call and find out!"

So the first mother calls her mother and asks her that same question.

"I don't know why I cut the end of the ham off. I did it because that's what *my* mother did. Let me call my mother and see if she can tell me why she cut the end off of the ham before cooking it."

So another call is made and the great-grandmother of the young girl who first posed the question answers her daughter.

"I cut the end off of the ham because if I didn't, it wouldn't fit in the pan!"

As a result, two generations of mothers are cutting off the end of a ham simply because one mother did it so it would fit in the cooking pan. The great-grandmother made a habit of cutting the end of the ham off out of necessity. Several generations of daughters copied that habit without any understanding of why they were doing it. This pattern of cooking was wired into the daughters' brains over time through repeated behavior. The pattern of behavior became automatic, and it was not until that pattern of behavior was questioned that the mothers realized the impact those modeled behaviors had on their own.

While this is a simplistic illustration, it helps us see just how blind we are to our behavior. Many of us have a morning routine and nighttime routine. Most of us do not even know what that routine is because we have done it so long we do not even think about it. In fact, we often have to pause to think about it in order to explain it to others. Some people eat one item of a meal first before they eat the next. For instance, they eat their chicken first, not eating their rice until their chicken is completely gone. Most people do not realize that they are doing this and often cannot explain *why* they started eating that way. The point, however, is that consistent behaviors get wired in the brain and become so automatic we do not even realize it.

Despite the resourcefulness of the brain, this plasticity is not all good news. While it has the power to produce a wonderfully flexible organ, the brain's plasticity can also work to create behaviors that are more rigid.[32] Once a particular plastic change takes place, it can inhibit other changes from occurring, thus hindering or preventing functional and structural modifications that allow behavioral change. One scientist calls this the "plastic paradox."[33]

## Experience and Plasticity

The various experiences of our environment work to bring about changes in the brain. The brain's "neural architecture comes to reflect the environment that shapes it."[34] The more enriched the environment, the greater the level of stimulation and complexity. This stimulation enhances learning and growth. Each unique stimulation adds a layer of experience to the brain, creating more complex responses to those experiences.[35] Stimulation and challenge are necessary for brain plasticity because they keep the brain from functioning only via its automatic processes.[36]

In one of the churches that I pastored, a family began coming to our church that home-schooled their two boys. There were several reasons for their homeschooling choice.

57

One reason was because they moved around quite a bit with the husband's job. One of the things I admired about how they educated their children was how they intentionally provided their boys with a variety of experiences. On the weekends, the family planned outings to museums, cultural centers, and outdoor activities. Part of their education during the week included trips to historical areas where they could see history, not just read about it. Even their dining choices were diverse and experience-oriented. As a result, the boys were incredibly gifted and creative. Though their personalities were different – one was quiet and reserved while the other was outgoing – their ability to conceptualize abstract concepts was amazing. They could create some of the most vivid and unique storylines I had ever heard.

Most importantly was their ability to adapt to new situations. Because they moved around a bit and had a variety of experiences, they were able to build relationships with a wide and diverse group of people. Obviously, they had habits as all of us do. Yet unlike those who struggle with change or new concepts, they had no problem learning, exploring or adapting to change because of the enriched environment they had growing up. An impoverished environment, however, with limited variation provides little stimulation or challenge. People with limited life experience find change and adaptation difficult.

**Thought and Brain Plasticity**

Science has discovered that "perception, sensation, and other subjective experiences reflect chemical and electrical changes in the brain. When electrical impulses zip through our visual cortex, we see, and when neurochemicals course through the limbic system, we feel – sometimes in response to an event in the outside world, sometimes as a result of a thought generated by the mind alone."[37] However, could the opposite be true? Is it possible that a person's thoughts could bring functional and structural changes to the brain?

The idea that only the brain acts on the brain is a philosophical view called "causal closure." This view states, "only the physical can act on the physical...But a nonphysical phenomenon is powerless to affect anything made out of tissues, molecules, and atoms."[38] However, in recent years, scientists are discovering that the mind, the rational, thinking areas of the brain, can affect the brain.

People with Obsessive-Compulsive Disorder (OCD), are "terrified that some harm will come, or has come, to them or to those they love."[39] These people are compulsive worriers. Those with OCD may attempt to get relief by focusing on what is worrying them.[40] For instance, if a person is germaphobic, he or she will try to make sure there is no possible way germs can reach him or her. She may install filters in one's home to keep from breathing in germs out of the air in addition to constantly washing her hands.

Unfortunately, the more she thinks about her fear, the more she worries about it.[41] When obsessive worrying begins, OCD patients will typically begin to do something to diminish the worry.[42] If, for instance, they *feel* germs have contaminated them when they touch something, they will wash their hands.[43] The action of washing their hands allows them to *feel* that they have removed the threat.

The brain of an OCD patient does not allow the person to move past the feeling of regret when making a mistake, and, as such, the person obsesses about the mistake. Scientists have discovered through brain scans that three areas of the brain are involved in obsessions.[44] The *orbital frontal cortex*, which lies just behind the eyes, is the brain region where mistakes are detected. When the "mistake feeling," that nagging sense that something is wrong,[45] is detected, it signals the *cingulate gyrus*, an integral part of the limbic system, which is involved with emotion formation and processing, learning and memory.[46] This, in turn, triggers the anxiety feeling that something bad will happen if the mistake is not corrected. The *caudate nucleus* is the part of a person's brain that allows thoughts to progress from one thought to the next unless, as in the case of OCD patients, the caudate becomes stuck. Scientists refer to this as brain lock.[47]

James Schwartz set out to develop a treatment that would allow patients to release this brain lock. The approach Schwartz developed actually creates a new brain circuit. The new circuit gives pleasure and triggers the release of dopamine, which "rewards the new activity and consolidates and grows new neural connections. The new circuit can eventually compete with the older one, and according to 'use it or lose it' theories, the pathological networks will weaken. With this treatment we don't so much 'break' bad habits as replace bad behaviors with better ones."[48]

Schwartz's therapy works in two stages. First, each time the patient feels an oncoming OCD attack, the person decides to think differently about the worrying by relabeling the worry. The patient thinks differently about his or her problem, noting that what he or she is experiencing is not an attack of, say germs or battery acid, but an episode of OCD. The patient reminds himself that what is happening is the result of a faulty circuit.[49] Second, the patient refocuses on something positive and pleasurable. By doing this, the patient fixes his or her transmission issues by growing and strengthening new circuits and altering the caudate.⁵⁰ "By not acting on the compulsion, patients weaken the link between the compulsion and the idea it will ease their anxiety."⁵¹ One principle of neuroplasticity states that "Neurons that fire together, wire together." The corollary is, "Neurons that fire apart, wire apart."⁵²

Schwartz has seen tremendous results from his work. Eighty percent of his patients get better with this method in combination with medication. The medication helps ease the anxiety that comes with obsessive-compulsive disorder, allowing the patients to integrate the therapy. In time, many of the patients are able to discontinue their medication.⁵³ In addition, in brain scans following therapy, the three areas of the brain that once were locked together show signs of firing separately as if the brain were normal.⁵⁴

Schwartz's conclusion was that "[t]herapy had altered the metabolism of the OCD circuit....This was the first study to show that cognitive behaviour therapy has the power to systematically change faulty brain chemistry in a well-identified brain circuit."⁵⁵ The brain changes showed that "willful, mindful effort can alter brain function, and that such self-directed brain changes – neuroplasticity – are a genuine reality."⁵⁶

Further evidence of the ability of thought to produce change can be found in a study done by researchers Guang Yue and Kelly Cole. Their study looked at two different groups of people. One group did physical exercise and the other group simply imagined doing the exercise. Both of the groups "exercised" a finger muscle five days per week for four consecutive weeks.⁵⁷ The group that physically exercised the finger muscle did

> fifteen maximal contractions, with a twenty second rest between each. The mental group merely imagined doing fifteen maximal contractions, with a twenty second rest between each, while also imagining a voice shouting at them, "Harder! Harder! Harder!"
>
> At the end of the study, the subjects who had done physical exercise increased their muscular strength by 30 percent, as one might expect. Those who only imagined doing the exercise, for the same period, increased the muscle strength by 22 percent. The explanation lies in the motor neurons of the brain that "program" movements. During those imaginary contractions, the neurons responsible for stringing together sequences of instructions for movements are activated and strengthened, resulting in increased strength when the muscles are contracted.[58]

From a neurological perspective, imagining an act and doing the act are not that different.

Repeatedly doing an action builds and reinforces neural circuits in the brain that control behavior. This makes it difficult to change our behavior because we have to break how these neural circuits are wired by creating and reinforcing new circuits leading to new patterns of behavior.

Accomplishing this means we have to heal our emotions so as to change our thinking. Since we act, however, out of our identity which is formed from our experiences and relationships, we essentially have to re-experience life. Wholeness requires that we set aside our old way of thinking, feeling, and acting while at the same time experiencing a new way of thinking, feeling, and acting. Doing so changes our identity, continually re-forming us into the image of Christ, in whose image we were created.

# THE CHANGE PROCESS

Richard Boyatzis and Annie McKee are professors who have looked at intentional behavioral change in the area of leadership. In their book, *Resonant Leadership*, the authors discuss the impact of resonance and renewal on leadership. Resonance "means that people's emotional centers are in synch in a positive way."[1] In addition, resonance is "the ability of leaders to perceive and influence the flow of emotions (including motivational states) between themselves and others they work with."[2] Resonant leaders work hard to develop emotional intelligence – self-awareness, self-management, social awareness, and relationship management. Not only do they have it in themselves, they manage an environment where others can manage their own emotions and build strong and trusting relationships.[3] However, sustaining this kind of leadership requires renewal, which the authors define as "developing practices – habits of mind, body and behavior – that enable us to create and sustain resonance in the face of unending challenges, year in and year out."[4]

According to Boyatzis and McKee, recently completed long-term research studies demonstrate that sustainable change takes place when we focus on five major discoveries:

- The *ideal self*, or what you would want out of life and the person you want to be – leading to your personal vision, the deepest expression of what we want in life.
- The *real self*, or how you act and are seen by others; the comparison of the real self to the ideal self results in identification of your strengths and weaknesses – leading to your personal balance sheet showing areas where the real self and ideal self are congruent and incongruent.
- Your *learning agenda* enables you to capitalize on your strengths and moves you closer to your personal vision while possibly working on a weakness or two (or working to maintain the ideal current state of your life and work).
- *Experimenting with and practicing new habits* or reinforcing and affirming your strengths.
- *Developing and maintaining close, personal relationships* – resonant relationships – that enable you to move through these discoveries toward renewal.[5]

These discoveries provide us insight into a biblical, holistic model of change.

The *ideal self* is a look at who we really are. The ideal self is our ideal identity. The ideal self is the *imago christi*, the image of Christ. This was the identity in which we were created to live. Looking at Christ, He was the human we were designed to be. Through repentance, we are found to be "in Christ" positionally, while at the same time we are journeying towards a wholeness that is found when we are "in Christ" relationally.

The *real self* is how we currently act and how we understand ourselves. We are broken people, acting out of an identity formed through others, experiences, and the general brokenness that accompanies a world filled with sinful, broken people. We act in unhealthy ways. We think destructive thoughts. We are hurting people trying to appease Garden longings. Uncovering our emotional health and noting the destructive habits provide us a starting point for our journey toward wholeness.

When we *experiment with and practice new habits*, we are engaging the process of neural rewiring. This rewiring process requires our engagement with spiritual disciplines and prayer all done in the context of a community of faith and through *close, personal relationships*. We also have to unlearn habits and put into place new behaviors that rewire our circuits, creating automatic processes and new behaviors.

The *learning agenda* is the journey on which the Spirit takes us to bring that journey to fruition. In the business world, we might plan a learning agenda that maximizes our strengths and allows us to work on our weaknesses in a systematic way. However, the Holy Spirit is the wind that powers our sails and takes us where He wants us to go, not where we want to go. The Spirit lays out our learning plan. We are pneumanauts, preparing for the divine leading instead of planning our own agendas. This means we are not in control; however, as Christians, we should understand we are not in control. And it is in letting go that we actually find great freedom as the blowing of the wind through our hearts takes us on our journey towards wholeness.

## THE DISCIPLINES AND COMMUNITY

We noted previously that spiritual disciplines are an important part of the journey towards wholeness. The disciplines and a faith community are the entryway to self-awareness, emotional healing, and thought change.

Discipline is not a popular term in our culture. It is a "radical call to a largely undisciplined and comfort-seeking culture."[1] It is a symptom of our drive for instant gratification. This instant fulfillment of needs and desires allows no time or energy for the long journey of discipline. However, it is the only way to begin the journey towards wholeness.

There is a danger. The practice of the disciplines can themselves be a symptom of brokenness. The disciplines can become a rigid structure of life that allows no room for the divine interruptions of life. The disciplines become a fixed order of being, and the possibilities of changes in the pattern becomes unthinkable. The disciplines for some can become the "total content of their relationship with God, and works righteousness, the shape of their spirituality."[2]

In the balance between no discipline and extreme discipline, however, the disciplines can be the avenue upon which our journey toward wholeness can travel. It is here that the potter God shapes us into the image of Christ.

Robert Mulholland, in his book *Invitation to a Journey* speaks well to this idea of the positive motives and impact of the classical spiritual disciplines. The classical spiritual disciplines are

> the practices that the church has come to realize are essential for deepening one's relationship with God, enriching one's life with others and nurturing one towards wholeness in Christ. While the classical spiritual disciplines, such as prayer, Bible reading, worship, study, fasting, retreat and daily office, have both personal and corporate dimensions, the personal disciplines are acts of loving obedience which we offer our brokenness and bondage to God for healing and liberation… Without the classical disciplines, personal disciplines can quickly become privatized and even pathological-privatized in the sense of keeping our relationship with God firmly under our control and permitting us to adjust the call to discipleship to fit our agenda, our likes and dislikes, our wants and wishes; pathological in the sense of a spirituality that binds us to inadequate or destructive responses to life. Without personal disciplines, on the other hand, the classical disciplines can quickly become a debilitating façade that covers one's deep needs for transformation. ³

In other words, personal change requires the interaction with the body of Christ. However, simply participating in the classical disciplines, while providing the *doing*, cannot lead to *being*.

According to Mulholland, we "tend to think of the classical spiritual disciplines of the body of Christ as secondary or even optional to the 'real' spirituality of our own private spiritual disciplines. But the classical disciplines serve to bring our lives into, and hold our lives in, God's environment for wholeness in Christ, so that the 'treatment' of our individual disciplines can be fully effective."[4] In addition, it is difficult to maintain genuine personal disciplines without the foundation of classical spiritual disciplines with the body of Christ. They give us support so that our personal spiritual disciplines can become the means whereby God can transform us into the image of Christ.

Let us now consider some essential aspects of the classical disciplines.

## Prayer

We tend to think of prayer as "something we *do* in order to produce the results we believe are needed, or rather, to get God to produce the results."[5] Our prayers tend to be shopping lists. It's our Christmas list to Santa Claus. I need. Please give. We treat it as a functional part of life.

Prayer, however, is relational as a classic spiritual discipline. The modern Catholic spiritual writer, Henry Nouwen expresses the idea of prayer effectively when he states:

> *In a situation in which the world is threatened by annihilation, prayer does not mean much when we undertake it only as an attempt to influence God, or as a search for a spiritual fallout shelter, or as an offering of comfort in stress-filled times...Prayer is the act by which we divest ourselves of all false belongings and become free to belong to God and God alone.*[6]

Prayer is a must for our relationship with God, particularly this kind of praying. However, it is not comfortable. Nouwen adds:

> *We want to move closer to God, the source and goal of our existence, but at the same time we realize that the closer we come to God the stronger will be his demand to let go of the many "safe" structures we have built around ourselves. Prayer is such a radical act because it requires us to criticize our whole way of being in the world, to lay down our old selves and accept our new self, which is Christ…Prayer therefore is the act of dying to all that we consider to be our own and of being born to a new existence which is not of the world.*[7]

This certainly transforms our thoughts about prayer, does it not? The shopping list prayers and manipulation types of prayers may simply be a way to avoid a deep relationship with God, to keep God at arm's length and keep God under our control. Yet prayer as a classical discipline "draws us into God's involvement in the brokenness of the world on God's terms, not ours."[8]

In the book of the Revelation, John sees this reality in his vision of the opening of the seventh symbol (Rev 8:1-5). Mulholland notes:

> *The images of the angel, the altar, the coals and the incense relate to the incense offering on the Day of Atonement in the temple in Jerusalem. The incense offering was the liturgical act that began the daily office of temple worship. Usually the priest selected to offer the incense offering was given a silver censer and about half a pound of incense. But on the Day of Atonement, the day on which the people of God were brought into full and perfect covenant relationship with God, the priest would be given a golden censer and as much*

> incense as he could hold. *The priest would then ascend the large sacrificial altar in the courtyard in front of the sanctuary. Upon this altar the sacrificial fire perpetually burned. The priest would scoop coals from the sacrificial fire into the censer and then descend from the altar. As he entered the sanctuary, he approached the Altar of Incense, the Golden Altar, which stood before the Holy of Holies, where God's presence was believed to dwell. He would place the coals on the altar and then drop the incense on the coals, and the smoke of the incense would rise into the presence of God in the Holy of Holies.*
>
> *In John's vision, the angel is given much incense to mingle with the prayers of the saints, another image that would have been familiar to Jewish Christians in the first century. The times of prayer in the synagogues were scheduled to coincide with the daily sacrifices at the temple in Jerusalem: prayer was associated with sacrifice. In John's vision, therefore, the prayers of the saints were mingled with the sacrificial fire of God's holiness in God's presence.*[9]

The vision provides us something new. The angel scoops up the prayers of the saints and hurls them onto the earth. The result is thunder, lightning, earthquakes, and voices – all images of God's disruptive presence in the world.

Using this metaphor, John provides us with a great representation about the nature of prayer. "Prayer is the act by which the people of God become incorporated into the presence and action of God in the world. Prayer becomes a sacrificial offering of ourselves to God, to become agents of God's presence and action in the daily events and situations of our lives."[10] Again, this offers us a more meaningful understanding of prayer.

This kind of prayer is difficult to practice as an individual. We need to pray with the body of Christ, others in our community of faith and in the church universal. We need this because corporate praying moves us out of the individual and personal nature of praying and gives us a broader, deeper understanding of a vital relationship with and sacrificial response to God. For this reason, Mulholland says we should make use of the prayers of the church that have come before us. We should make use of the Psalms as our prayer book. "This is the essence of the classical spiritual discipline of prayer: not our private, individualized prayers, but immersing ourselves in the deep, sacrificial prayers of the saints through which the church through the ages has offered itself to be the body of Christ in the world. Unless our individual prayer life exists within the greater support structure of the prayers of the saints, it will tend to become very narrow, individualized and privatized, and we will shy away from yielding control of our existence for God's purposes."[11]

I currently do not participate in reading and praying the prayers of the saints long ago. I do read at least one Psalm during my devotional time. However, I have used a prayer book in the past. Phyllis Tickle has a whole series of books called *The Divine Hours*, which offers fixed hour prayers that coincide with the time of the prayers of the early Christians. There is an Old Testament, New Testament, and Psalm text for each day along with prayers of the saints throughout the years. I combined this with prayers for friends and family and found the prayer experience entirely refreshing.

At first, I thought this type of praying to be odd. I had only known prayer in the context of supplication and intercession.

Growing up a Baptist, I never used a prayer book or a lectionary. It was foreign to me. However, a friend, along with an author I read and respect, suggested this practice. Reading and praying aloud the prayers of others and of the Psalms is a humbling experience. It also does exactly what Mulholland suggests: it removes prayer from the "bless me", "help me", and "help others" focus to a relational, historical, and global focus.

Interestingly, Baptists do use responsive readings, which in past hymnals are found in the back of those hymnals. That has been a healthy and, at times, awe-inspiring experience. To hear the voices of the church read aloud a Psalm, a prayer or a scripture, or to hear them respond aloud to a challenge from scripture can be a profound experience. Sadly, we do not practice it enough.

## Spiritual Reading

Spiritual reading "is the discipline of openness to encounter God through the writings of the mothers and fathers of the church, beginning with the scriptures."[12] In spiritual reading, the text opens us up to God's control of our daily lives for his purposes. A time of spiritual reading is entered into when the text is chosen for us, Mulholland believes. The lectionary can be an example of this. In letting the text be chosen for us, we begin by actually yielding control over to someone or something else. This allows the text to have control over us and be a place where we encounter God. [13] This keeps us from simply trying to gain information from the text.

Pastors and teachers, specifically, are in danger of reading the scriptures in an informational way. Always concerned about the next sermon or the next lecture, we can move our scripture reading from a time when the text challenges us to a time when we are objectifying the text, trying to see how we can best utilize it for our purposes.

Spiritual reading has as its classical expression the *Lectio Divina*.[14] The classical form of the *lectio divina* has four components: *lectio, mediatio, oratio* and *contemplatio*. Mulholland adds to this an introductory period of *silancio* along with a concluding component called the *incarnatio*. *Silancio* is a period of silence before reading the text and *incarnatio* is the reader living out the text.

The basics of the *lectio divina* begins with the reader reading the texts, often several times. This is the *lectio*. The act of meditating on the text, whereby the reader processes what he or she has read is the *mediato*. The *oratio* is the element where the reader responds to God based on what he or she has read. This can be a verbal response such as singing or praying aloud, or a non-verbal response such as journaling. The final element of the *lectio*, the *contemplatio*, "moves us into a posture of released waiting on God for whatever reason God wants to do in us, with us, through us."[15] It is a period of time where we sit and contemplate what we have read and wait on God.

All of these are strange to our culture. We are so busy that the time requirements to complete the practice of *lectio divina* are beyond many of us. The thought of spending more than five minutes in reading, meditating, and responding to the scriptures is foreign to us. In avoiding this practice, we are not letting the scriptures "teach us what is true and to make us realize what is wrong in our lives."[16]

If we limit our interaction with the scriptures, we are not letting God open the entryway of our transformational change process. We are not allowing ourselves to begin the journey.

*The Disciplines and Community*

This is because the scriptures, along with our relationships, reveal our emotional brokenness, the patterns of destructive thinking and habits as well as areas where we are hurting others. For instance, the morning I wrote this chapter, I read Psalm 15 from *The Message*. In this chapter, David wonders aloud who may enter into the house of God. Part of the response included "Keep your word even when it costs you, make an honest living".[17] I paused over this verse. I run a couple of businesses in addition to being a pastor. I took the time to consider if I have recently not kept my word (and I have) or if I have cheated anyone in my business practices (which I haven't). The first thing I did was confess the sin and ask for forgiveness. Then I took the extra time to consider the bigger and more important question of *why* I did not keep my word. Did I not want to keep my word, and if so, why? Did I simply forget? If so, was this a one-time thing or a continuing practice specifically with this person? In addition, what practices do I need to put into place to keep this from happening again?

This practice of letting the text challenge us to explore the motivation behind behavior are keys to opening up the emotional brokenness and the destructive thinking that help free us towards a life of wholeness as well as conformity to the image of Christ.

# EMOTIONAL HEALING

Based on what we have seen in an earlier chapter, we are primarily emotional people. If that is true, then when we look at the Scriptures, we will find that our brokenness results in sins that are primarily emotional. Our sinful behavior is emotionally based.

One clear example of this comes from Galatians 5. Paul states in 5:16-22:

> So I say, let the Holy Spirit guide your lives. Then you won't be doing what your sinful nature craves. The sinful nature wants to do evil, which is just the opposite of what the Spirit wants. And the Spirit gives us desires that are the opposite of what the sinful nature desires. These two forces are constantly fighting each other, so you are not free to carry out your good intentions. But when you are directed by the Spirit, you are not under obligation to the law of Moses.
>
> When you follow the desires of your sinful nature, the results are very clear: sexual immorality, impurity, lustful pleasures, idolatry, sorcery, hostility, quarreling, jealousy, outbursts of anger, selfish ambition, dissension, division, envy, drunkenness, wild parties, and other sins like these.

## Emotional Healing

*Let me tell you again, as I have before, that anyone living that sort of life will not inherit the Kingdom of God.*

*But the Holy Spirit produces this kind of fruit in our lives: love, joy, peace, patience, kindness, goodness, faithfulness, gentleness, and self-control. There is no law against these things! (NLT)*

Notice two key words here: crave and desires. These are emotional words, not rational or logical words. The desires we were born with express themselves in emotional ways: anger, selfishness, envy, hostility, and lust. The desires that the Spirit gives us are emotional words as well: love, peace, patience, kindness, gentleness, etc. The journey towards wholeness takes place when the Spirit replaces our broken emotions that express a discontent with ourselves, others, and God with healthy emotions that express a person's life "in Christ". We live out of our emotions so to bring wholeness we need emotional healing.

This is why we need the disciplines mentioned in the previous chapter. When we meditate on scripture, we allow the Holy Spirit to bring to mind the motivation for our behavior, which will be emotional. Let us look at an example.

Suppose you are reading the scripture above and God, through the Spirit causes you to pause on the phrase, "outbursts of anger". You begin to ponder questions such as: What is the source of my outbursts? What caused me to erupt in an angry manner?

Imagine that you erupted angrily because someone unintentionally cut you off on the highway. Maybe you blew the horn, slammed your hand on the dash, or yelled at them. It is possible you do all three. Why? Is it because someone took your spot in the traffic train? Why would get you upset to not be a few feet farther up the road? Is it that important?

What essentially happened is that someone either took something that you feel is yours (a place on the highway) or put you in harm's way by almost hitting you with his car. You had an emotional reaction to not getting your way or being in danger. Regardless, that emotional reaction may have resulted from some memory, one that as we have seen, you may not even realize, or fear in general.

In Isaiah 51:9-16, the prophet shares an urgent appeal to God that He act quickly. The appeal is for God to mobilize his strength. The inference is that God was asleep during the part of Israel's history when they were taken away into captivity. If God would wake up, the trouble the captives had with Babylon would be over because no power can withstand God's strong arm.

Yahweh responds in the first person to offer assurance to the people. God's first person assurance of "I am he who comforts you" is followed by a rebuke. He questions why the people were afraid of a mortal who will die, a human who will fade away. Through their fear, they had forgotten God. God had not been asleep; the people had been so afraid of their captives that they had forgotten Yahweh. Old Testament scholar Walter Brueggemann states,

> *The reason Israel fears such a one is that Israel has forgotten the decisive difference Yahweh makes. The implication is that adherence to Yahweh will veto any trouble from Babylon. The reason is that Yahweh, according to Israel's doxology, is creator not only of Israel but of earth and heaven. Yahweh has all power, contrasted with his "mere mortal" who has no real power, has created*

> nothing, and therefore need not be feared or obeyed. Israel, in its deep, weak-willed forgetfulness, however, is mesmerized by "the oppressor," endlessly aware of the danger of the oppressor, and therefore prone to obey that one instead of Yahweh, its proper object of trust and obedience.[1]

That emotion, fear, kept the people of God from hearing, obeying, and relating to the one who made them. Fear is that powerful. In other words, an emotion determined their behavior and their allegiance. Emotions are that powerful. That is why we must deal with them.

## Dealing with our Emotions

Psychologists Leslie Greenberg and Sandra Paivio outline a process of dealing with the influence our emotions have on us. The process requires that the person confront his emotional pain rather than avoid it. The person needs to re-experience the emotions and feelings associated with emotional memories so that he or she can understand them and accept them as being a part of life.[2] By "re-owning" experiences, the person understands he has a right to the resulting emotions. Once a person acknowledges and experiences the pain of an emotion, he can develop hope.[3] "Hope develops, from the sense that 'It is I who is feeling this, it is me [sic] who is an agent in this feeling' and then 'It is me [sic] who can do something about this.' A sense of agency is created by recognizing oneself as a creator or author of one's experience. While a sense of agency may not yet provide a concrete plan of action, there is a feeling of confidence that action is possible and that change can occur."[4]

As a person experiences hope, he becomes excited about

the possible future. He generally believes that a future where his life is different is obtainable. Hope engages the spirit and raises the energy level, causing the person to act. "Hope is an emotional magnet – it keeps people going even in the midst of challenges...Hope binds people together and helps us move in concert toward a desired end."[5]

Hope believes that there is a chance for a future that is positively different from how we live and act today. Sadly, most of us have tried so often to change our behavior that we have exhausted any hope of that happening. This is because we have bypassed the most important step of emotional healing.

That hope, however, must not be misplaced hope, for misdirected hope leaves us hopeless. The hope that can transform us is not hope in ourselves or hope in another person. Hope is found only in Christ. Nevertheless, like so many aspects of relationships, hope must be developed. It is a process. The apostle Paul reminds us of this in Romans 5:1-5:

> *Therefore, since we have been made right in God's sight by faith, we have peace with God because of what Jesus Christ our Lord has done for us. Because of our faith, Christ has brought us into this place of undeserved privilege where we now stand, and we confidently and joyfully look forward to sharing God's glory.*
>
> *We can rejoice, too, when we run into problems and trials, for we know that they help us develop endurance. And endurance develops strength of character, and character strengthens our confident hope of salvation. And this hope will not lead to disappointment. For we know how dearly God loves us, because he has given us the Holy Spirit to fill our hearts with his love. (NLT)*

Present Christian experience is not only one of peace with God but of suffering. This suffering, however, is to be understood as part of a larger storyline that ends with hope. Paul had points of connection with this historically and experientially. While there was a wilderness before the Israelites entered the Promised Land, despite the long journey and difficult journey, God provided for the community and kept his promise. He was faithful to the promise he made to Abram over four hundred years earlier in Genesis 15, despite the moments of faithlessness of the people.

Paul knew what it was like to go through difficult times. He had been beaten, left for dead, thrown in prison, and shipwrecked. Those experiences did not weaken his hope; they solidified his hope. Paul went on to say in 2 Corinthians 4:7-12:

> *We've been surrounded and battered by troubles, but we're not demoralized; we're not sure what to do, but we know that God knows what to do; we've been spiritually terrorized, but God hasn't left our side; we've been thrown down, but we haven't broken. What they did to Jesus, they do to us—trial and torture, mockery and murder; what Jesus did among them, he does in us—he lives! Our lives are at constant risk for Jesus' sake, which makes Jesus' life all the more evident in us. While we're going through the worst, you're getting in on the best! (The Message)*

In the Christian context, that is the purpose of difficult times. Sufferings, struggles, and times of testing put stress on our life, and that stress reveals our heart. Our emotions are revealed, creating an opportunity not only to demonstrate how those emotions drive our behavior but what circumstances trigger that behavior. If we can uncover the experience, we can release the experience, providing emotional healing. The experience does not control us any more. God's enemy, Satan, cannot use that pain to manipulate us or deceive us any more. In that, confidence in Christ grows and our hope grows.

It has another impact. Others are unable tp manipulate us. The testing and trials develop endurance, or patience, Paul says. Patience reflects the idea of staying put without dismay. It is contentment not with ourselves or our situation, but contentment in the one who has placed us in that situation. That patience then develops strength of character, a character that makes Jesus' life all the more evident in us. As character develops, people are unable to guilt us into action. They cannot push our buttons. Character gives us a foundation of living that allows us to put in place boundaries that keep emotional manipulation from occurring.

# REWIRING THE BRAIN

When we have confronted our emotional memories, we offer ourselves the opportunity to consider our reaction to those emotions. We are free from the pain, and are able to respond, not react. Rather than an emotional reaction that we do not understand, we can inhibit the automatic reaction and make the best decision – if we choose to. This allows us to think clearly without the distortion from a difficult experience. Clarity of thought allows us to think differently. Thinking differently allows us to rewire those neural paths we discussed in a previous chapter. If we can do this, we can change the automatic processes already wired in our brain and rewire into our mind new automatic processes that reflect the behavior that exhibits a whole and healthy life. It is then that we can think for change.

## Part of My Journey

I spent much of my childhood as a latchkey kid. Both parents worked. Thirty years ago, it was acceptable to leave your kids at home by themselves for a few hours, so beginning around age nine I would take the bus home and wait for my parents to come home a couple of hours later. As with most kids, I would come home and get a snack. The snack depended on what was in the house at the time. Sometimes it would be a snack cake and at other times something leftover from last night's meal. I would eat that food while being entertained by *The Three Stooges*, or *The Little Rascals* or *Bugs Bunny*.

Up until recently, if I would come home from the office or from being out and about, the first thing I would do would be to open the refrigerator or the pantry to see what I might have for a snack. Those habits engrained within my life from elementary school stayed with me for almost thirty years. In fact, I never realized this was happening until I was forced to write down what I ate and when I ate it. It was then that I saw the pattern. It did not matter that I may have eaten an hour or so before. What I wired into my brain was that when I came home, I looked for food.

Changing that behavior required me to break the circuit that created the automatic processes that caused me to look for food when I came home in the afternoon. I had to intentionally come home and do something different from checking for food.

Other issues require similar behavior. For some time, when I would wake up in the morning I would go to the computer, check email, read blog posts from my blog reader and maybe make a blog post or two myself. Then it would be time to get to the office or a meeting of some kind and I would end up rushing to take a shower and get somewhere on time. It also meant that my daily worship time was often delayed until the afternoon, assuming that I did not have meetings or events scheduled for that time. In those cases, I may not even get to my daily worship time with God at all.

That behavior had to change. I engaged in that behavior for so long that it became automatic. I did not even realize that I was wiring a circuit that would lead to potentially addictive behavior. Rewiring the behavior meant that I needed to unlearn one behavior and learn another behavior.

Unlearning my computer addiction behavior meant that I had to consistently change the way I acted when I woke up. I had to make a conscious decision to get up in the morning and move to my place of daily worship. I had to be intentional about it. Over the course of a month, I was able to make that the normal part of waking up. Thinking differently over time caused me to act differently. Once you unlearn and learn a new behavior and make that automatic, you can start on a different behavior. More on that in a moment.

**Rewiring the circuits**

There are no simple solutions to rewiring our brain. Quitting a habit or changing a behavior can require an enormous amount of energy. It can also require the pain of others' disapproval. Marsha, for instance, had tried to quit smoking many times. She had seen a hypnotist, a therapist, and a doctor, but she still smoked two packs per day. Her husband and kids promised they would help her, but their promises were half-hearted. As soon as she became irritable, the family pushed her to go back to her regular self. Since Marsha used cigarettes to deal with her anxiety, going back to her regular self included smoking again. Changing her behavior would mean not only confronting the emotional aspects of her anxiety, but also dealing with her family. She would have to deal with their attempt to stifle her irritability that arose from leaving a nicotine addition.

## Countering

For decades, countering has been shown to be one of the most powerful processes in helping deal with a known habit. Countering is "substituting healthy responses for problem behaviors."[1] Undesirable behaviors have benefits. For instance, they help us cope with our emotional distress. When we try to change a habit or behavior, part of our journey could mean we have to replace that undesirable behavior with another behavior. When you remove troubled behaviors without healthy substitutes, "the risk of returning to old patterns remains high. Countering finds preferable substitutes."[2]

### Countering techniques

Research has given us at least five countering techniques that have proven to be successful in changing behavior. The first is active diversion. This is the most common, healthy alterative for problem behaviors.[3] Active diversion involves refocusing your energy, finding an enjoyable behavior that precludes the problem behavior. The possibilities for these behaviors are endless. You could clean, play the piano, read a book, go for a walk, or work in the yard. Recently, I was able to refocus some energy by building a standing desk from materials I had in our basement. This refocusing was a nice, physically challenging task that also required me to be creative in the use of materials as well as how I put the desk together.

Another technique is exercise. There is perhaps no more beneficial substitute for undesirable behaviors than exercise. "Omitting exercise from a … change plan is like fighting a foe with one hand tied behind your back. You may still win, but the odds are against you. Inactive people are not only in poor condition for dealing with physical problems, they are frequently also in poor psychological condition for coping with the distress that can accompany change."[4] The benefits of exercise are numerous:

- Improved body image, self-image, and self-esteem
- Increased energy, metabolism, and heart function
- Increased endorphins (self-produced painkillers)
- Decreased anxiety and depression
- Decreased body fat and cholesterol
- Decreased physical and emotional pain[5]

While some of these benefits can be gained from nonaerobic exercising such as walking, golf, or tennis, "the maximum return on your time is achieved by exercising at your aerobic threshold for twenty minutes."[6]

Still another countering technique that is effective is *relaxation*. There are times with exercise is not possible. The workday is tense and you may feel the need to eat or grab a cigarette, but going out for a jog is not possible. Relaxation can help in these times.

Deep relaxation has been shown to produce a mildly altered physical and mental state. Ten to twenty minutes of deep relaxation each day can give you:

- Increased energy
- Increased rate of alpha (pleasurable brain waves)
- Decreased blood pressure and muscle tension
- Decreased anxiety
- Improved sleep
- Improved health
- Improved concentration[7]

There are many ways to practice relaxation. I have an mp3 file on my mp3 player that has background music over which a person says, "Relax, just relax". When I would use this to help me relax, I would close my eyes and lay on my bed and just listen. Combined with good breathing techniques, this twenty minute practice every day would put me in a state to deal with the day, the issues of the day, and my own emotions and concerns. I also have several albums of quiet, relaxing music playing throughout the day or that I listen to on my mp3 player when I am stressed. Other techniques to help with relaxation include prayer, meditation, and yoga.

The fourth countering technique *is counterthinking*. Just as exercise replaces healthy behavior for unhealthy, counterthinking "replaces troubled thoughts with more positive ones."[8] This practice is quick, covert, takes little energy and can be used in almost all conditions that trigger undesirable behavior.

We need counterthinking because often our "self-talk" can trigger behavior. For instance, recently, I had a shipment of books that needed to be sent to a person in Minnesota. I was using a third party to develop and ship the books and had arranged for them to be shipped overnight. However, I knew I was dealing with a limited window for the printing of the books. When I went to bed the night before the books were to be delivered, I still did not know if they had been shipped. I lay in bed and began to sense anxiety developing. Then I started thinking through the implications of those books not getting delivered. I began to process the people I would be on the phone with and begin to complain to. In the past, I would get so worked up with what *might* happen that I couldn't sleep. I could feel my blood pressure rise. My muscles would tighten up. The anticipation of that frustration, my "self-talk", would put me in what my wife would call a "grumpy" state of being.

On this night, however, I recognized the thoughts, prayed, and reminded myself that I had done everything I could possibly do to get these books to Minnesota. I turned over, and quickly went to sleep. When I awoke the next morning, I discovered that the distributor shipped the books in time and they arrived when they needed to arrive. This is counterthinking. Counterthinking allows you to ask the question, "What am I telling myself that is getting me so upset?"[9] Often, our thinking is much worse than what actually is.

Often, our self-talking leads us into a state of depression or anxiety. What are some ways to deal with our self-talking? A great way is to memorize scripture. When we memorize scripture, we are more easily reminded of the words of the one in whose image we were created and the one in whose image we are being formed into. They remind us who we are in Christ, the provision of God when times are difficult, and give us wisdom at anxious moments. Another way to manage this is to have an encouraging book around to read. Another idea is to have positive sayings memorized or on small cards that you can access when necessary. Changing your thinking is not easy, but the repeatedly practicing counterthinking can expand your capacity for dealing with undesirable habits and behaviors.[10]

The fifth countering practice that helps in changing behavior is assertiveness. Problem behaviors can be triggered, and supported by other people in your life as well as by internal forces. Often we feel as though we are helpless to deal with the external forces that trigger or support our undesirable habits and behaviors. By being assertive, we express our right to communicate our thoughts, feelings, wishes, and intentions clearly, countering the feelings of helplessness.[11]

Assertiveness is a practice that you can use whenever "you

feel you are not being heard or respected."[12] There are benefits to you personally in being assertive. When you are assertive, you have:

- Decreased anxiety, anger, and neuroses
- Increased self-respect, communication, and leadership abilities
- Increased satisfaction in all personal relationships[13]

Most people can be assertive. However, many are not because they do not feel they have the right to be powerful. You need to realize that in relationships, you have:

- The right to be heard
- The right influence other people
- The right to make mistakes
- The right to change your mind
- The right to resist other people's judgments
- The right to have limits – limited knowledge, limited caring, limited responsibility for others, and limited time
- The right to have your limits respected[14]

In accepting and acting upon these rights, you are more likely to be assertive. In addition, when you acknowledge that other people have these same rights, "you will not confuse assertion with aggression. If nonassertive, passive behavior says that 'you count, but I don't,' and aggressive behavior says that 'I count, and you don't,' assertiveness respectfully communicates that 'I count just as your do.'"[15] It is important to note the distinctions. Assertion "does not accomplish goals at the expense of another person, as aggression does, nor does it deny your own rights, as does passivity. Rather, assertiveness grants all parties their rights."[16] This is the power of being a

Christ-differentiated person.

This does not mean that other people will honor, accept or approve your feelings or requests. If fact, it may create difficulty for you. Assertiveness assures that others will have the opportunity to understand your objectives, and therefore you will have increased your chances of meeting those objectives.[17]

## Environmental Control

You can do all the countering possible in the world, but if you go to a fast-good restaurant every time you are hungry, it will be difficult to control your weight. If you say yes to every project at the office, it will be hard to avoid overworking. Countering changes a person's response to a situation. Environmental control changes the situation itself. Both are necessary to change habits that rewire the brain.

Environmental change "involves restructuring your environment so that the likely occurrence of a problematic stimulus significantly reduced."[18] Let me go back to my computer addiction that I mentioned before. Not only did I have the issue in the morning, but also during the day I could sit at the computer involved in social media for long periods of time. I would get nothing done. One simple change I made was to get a simple program for my computer that allows me to create different kids of activities that would hide specific, distracting programs and block distracting websites for a designated period of time. For instance, I created a writing task that allows me to have only the programs I need to write open, plus my mp3 player for writing music, which also blocks access to social media sites and my email for one hour. I am able to work in a short, undistracted block of time, which helps me to also manage my ADD!

Another productivity buster for me is the television. Since I work in my home office a lot, the temptation to turn on the television and just see what is on is great. Sadly, my intended fifteen minutes often would turn into an hour or two without me even realizing how long I had been watching. I now have another office. It is Starbucks. I wrote much of this book sitting in Starbucks for hours at a time. I wrote much of my doctoral dissertation at a Panera Bread across the street from a university. I am a people person who needs to be around people. I do not have to talk to people per se, just be around them. It is an energy boost for me. Working at a coffee shop or café accomplishes two things for me: I am around people and I am able to not be around a television. In controlling my environment in this way, I am able to be more productive. At the same time, I am rewiring my neural circuits by putting into practice new behaviors and habits. I am finding that I am now able to write for longer periods of time, often not even recognizing that an hour has passed. There are many times when I do not even start the software that helps with my distractions.

### Rewards

Rewards modify the consequences that follow and reinforce behavior. Behavior that is celebrated or rewarded gets repeated. Rewards would not be needed if resisting temptation were its own reward. If a peach Snapple, which I consider the nectar of the gods, were not so good, I would not want to drink a case of it at one sitting. I do not find coffee to be tasty, so I do not have a problem with drinking it. In fact, I don't drink it at all. I've tried it every way I know. Suffice to say, I'm not addicted to coffee!

## Rewiring the Brain

Engaging in positive behavior needs to rewarded. When you sense a behavior trigger coming on but capture the thought and set it aside, not engaging in the undesirable behavior, give yourself a pat on the back. When you go to the gym instead of the couch, set aside a dollar to purchase new clothes for when you lose that excess weight.

By rewarding yourself, you change your self-talk. Your statements will now sound like the reminders that come from positive role models, parents or coaches, or teachers that consistently encouraged you to feel good about yourself and to do your best. It is as though you are "reparenting" yourself, learning more mature behavior and have more mature thoughts.

Countering, environmental controls, and rewards all facilitate the rewiring of our neural circuits. By creating new patterns of behavior, we see new circuits form. Then, by not using the old circuits, their synaptic strength degrades, resulting in reducing the frequency with which they will they fire together. With that, we begin to see the behavior that we found destructive gradually be minimized, if not eliminated altogether.

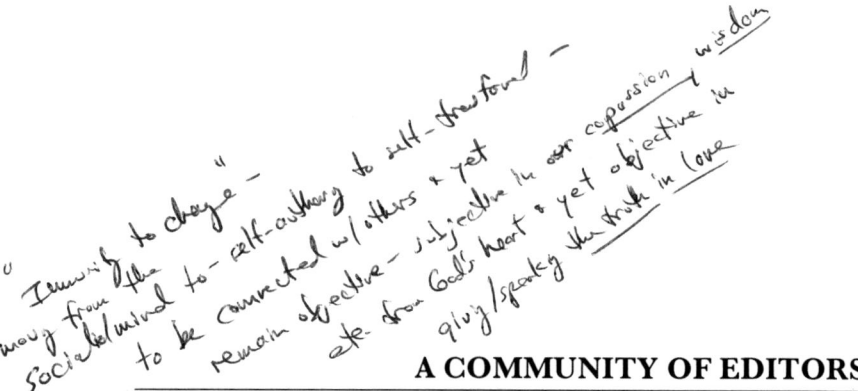

## A COMMUNITY OF EDITORS

We are wired to connect.

We know that instinctively.

Neuroscience is teaching us that our brain's design makes it sociable, drawn into an intimate brain-to-brain linkup whenever we interact with another person. This linkup is a neural bridge that affects the brain – and by extension the body – of everyone we interact with. Just as they do us. With every interaction.[1]

Routine encounters affect our brain. They prime our emotions, sometimes in desirable ways and sometimes in undesirable ways. These encounters operate as modulators, interpersonal thermostats that continually reset key aspects of our brain functions as they orchestrate our emotions. The feelings that result have great consequences, affecting everything from emotions to biological systems that regulate our hearts and immune cells. This brain to brain link "allows our strongest relationships to shape us on matters as benign as whether we laugh at the same jokes or as profound as which genes are (or are not) activated in T-cells, the immune system's foot soldiers in constant battle against invading bacteria and viruses."[2]

The social brain wires us for social interactions. These

interactions play a role in reshaping our brain through neuroplasticity. This means, "our key relationships can gradually mold certain neural circuitry. In effect, being chronically hurt and angered, or being emotionally nourished, by someone we spend time with daily over the course of years can refashion our brain."³ By refashioning our brain, we refashion our behavior.

*[Margin notes: we affect each other, for better or worse — words have power, of life or death — a bris, actions, because the "aroma of Christ or the scent of death"]*

## Socially Transforming Neighborhoods

During the 1990's, an economic upturn largely led to a nationwide downturn in crime rates. However, apart from broad forces, one researcher set out to discover if weaving people together would reduce crime on a particular block. Psychiatrist Felton Earls of Harvard undertook a ten-year study, one of the largest analyses of community involvement and crime done. Earls, along with his research team, made videos of 1,408 blocks of street life in 196 Chicago neighborhoods, including the poorest and most crime-ridden. They documented everything that occurred on these blocks. The tapes were then compared to crime records for these same neighborhoods, as well as with interviews from 8,782 neighborhood residents.⁴

The group found two primary influences on a neighborhood's crime rate. The first is the overall level of poverty. High poverty rates have been known for some time to spike crime. The second is the degree of connection among the people in a community. "The mix of poverty and disconnection, in tandem, exert a stronger influence over an area's crime rates than the standard factors usually cited, including race, ethnic background, or family structure."⁵

*[Margin note: of course!]*

Earls found that even in the poorest neighborhoods,

"positive personal connections were associated not just with lower crime rates but also with less drug use among young people, fewer unwanted pregnancies, and a rise in children's academic performance."6

**A Look in the Mirror**

In 1992, neuroscientists were mapping the sensorimotor area of monkeys' brains. During this research, something unexpected happened. One hot afternoon a research assistant came back from a break eating an ice-cream cone. The scientists saw something amazing happen. When the assistant lifted the cone to his lips, a sensorimotor cell activated in a monkey's brain. A distinct set of neurons seemed to activate when the monkey simply watched another monkey or experimenter make a movement. Since that finding, those same systems have been found in the human brain. They are called mirror neurons.7

Mirror neurons do what they suggest. They reflect back an action we observe in someone else. They actually cause us to mimic that action or at least have the impulse to mimic that action. It explains the lyrics to *When You're Smiling*, a song first recorded by Louis Armstrong in 1929:

> *When you're smiling*
> *When you're smiling*
> *The whole world smiles with you*
>
> *When you're laughing*
> *When you're laughing*
> *The sun comes shining through*
>
> *But when you're crying*

*You bring on the rain*
*So stop your sighing*
*Be happy again*

*Keep on smiling*
*Cause when you're smiling*
*The whole world smiles with you*

"to mourn w/ those who mourn, to rejoice..."

    Mirror neurons are adjacent to the motor neurons. This means that simply by their location, "the areas of the brain that initiate a movement can readily begin to activate even as we watch someone else make that same movement."[8] It not only helps initiate actions, it helps read intentions and emotions. For instance, if a person lays in a functional MRI machine watching a video showing someone smile or look angry, most of the brain areas activated in the person watching the video are the same brain areas activated by the one who was actually recorded making the facial expressions, though not as extreme. Therefore, mirror neurons are what make emotions contagious.[9] They ensure that generally, "the moment someone sees an emotion expressed" on a face, that person will at once sense that same feeling within himself or herself.[10]

    The apostle Paul reminded the people of Corinth to be aware of those they allowed to have influence over their lives. He said to this first century church, "Don't be fooled by those who say such things, for 'bad company corrupts good character.'"[11] Paul understood intuitively what science is now teaching us: we act and feel like those we watch and observe. Through mirror neurons, we begin to construct neural scaffolding upon which our behaviors are wired and modeled.

our subjective, broken response outside of a Spirit-filled, objective response!

## The Loss of Community

Unfortunately, social interactions are on the decline in Western culture. In 1995, Robert Putnam wrote an article in the *Journal of Democracy* entitled "Bowling Alone: America's Declining Social Capital". He later expanded this into a book entitled *Bowling Alone: The Collapse and Revival of American Community*. In the book, he argued that civil society was breaking down as Americans became more disconnected from their families, neighbors, communities, and the republic itself. The organizations that gave life to democracy were fraying. Bowling became his driving metaphor. Years ago thousands of people belonged to bowling leagues. Today, however, they're more likely to bowl alone. Television, two-career families, suburban sprawl, generational changes in values—these and other changes in American society have meant that fewer and fewer of us find that the League of Women Voters, or the United Way, or the Shriners, or the monthly bridge club, or even a Sunday picnic with friends fits the way we have come to live. Our growing social-capital deficit threatens educational performance, safe neighborhoods, equitable tax collection, democratic responsiveness, everyday honesty, and even our health and happiness.

A 2006 study for *American Sociological Review* reminds us again of the lack of disconnect we have with others. According to a report in USAToday:

> *Americans have a third fewer close friends and confidants than just two decades ago — a sign that people may be living lonelier, more isolated lives than in the past.*
>
> *In 1985, the average American had three people in whom to confide matters that were important to them, says a study in*

*today's American Sociological Review. In 2004, that number dropped to two, and one in four had no close confidants at all.*[12]

It is not only an issue in the United States. Research commissioned for the BBC found that UK society is a far lonelier one over the last 30 years (1971-2001), noting that "neighbourhoods in every part of the UK have become more socially fragmented."[13]

Daniel Dorling of Sheffield University headed the research team which created a formula based on "the proportion of people in an area who are single, those who live alone, the numbers in private rented accommodation and those who have lived there for less than a year....The higher the proportion of people in those categories, the less rooted the community, according to social scientists. They refer to it as the level of 'anomie' or the 'feeling of not belonging'."[14]

Using these measures, they found that the weakest communities in 1971 were stronger than the strongest communities in 2001. An astonishing 97% of neighborhoods had experienced this increased isolation over these 30 years.

The researchers conclude that "the increase in anomie weakens the 'social glue' of communities. The result, they suggest, is that neighbourhoods are likely to be less trusting and more fearful."[15]

The implications of community are broad. Putnam was able to demonstrate:

- Child development is powerfully shaped by social capital. Trust, networks, and norms of reciprocity within a child's family, school, peer group, and larger community have far reaching effects on their opportunities and choices, educational

achievement, and hence on their behavior and development.
- In high social-capital areas public spaces are cleaner, people are friendlier, and the streets are safer. Traditional neighborhood "risk factors" such as high poverty and residential mobility are not as significant as most people assume. Places have higher crime rates in large part because people don't participate in community organizations, don't supervise younger people, and aren't linked through networks of friends.
- A growing body of research suggests that where trust and social networks flourish, individuals, firms, neighborhoods, and even nations prosper economically. Social capital can help to mitigate the insidious effects of socioeconomic disadvantage.
- There appears to be a strong relationship between the possession of social capital and better health. As a rough rule of thumb, if you belong to no groups but decide to join one, you cut your risk of dying over the next year in half. If you smoke and belong to no groups, it is a toss-up statistically whether you should stop smoking or start joining. Regular club attendance, volunteering, entertaining, or church attendance is the happiness equivalent of getting a college degree or more than doubling your income. Civic connections rival marriage and affluence as predictors of life happiness.[16]

Social capital also has an impact on our happiness.

Richard Layard argued that seven factors are central to happiness. Furthermore, he used research such as the US General Social Survey to establish (for the US at least) five factors in some sort of order of importance. Two further factors were seen as central, but could not be ranked due to lack of survey evidence. The factors include:

1. Family relationships. In just about every study, family relationships and our close private life are 'more important than any other single factor affecting our happiness'.[17]
2. Financial situation. The individual financial position is of significance - especially when we are on the margins of poverty - but beyond that, it is a poor second to the quality of close and family relationships as a significant source of longish term happiness.
3. Work. There is considerable evidence that we need to feel we are contributing to the wider society. Layard comments, "[W]ork provides not only income but also an extra meaning to life". He continues "That is why unemployment is such a disaster: it reduces income but it also reduces happiness directly by destroying the self-respect and social relationships created by work".[18] However, it is also that the work is fulfilling (and here one of the most significant features is the degree of control people have over what they do).[19]
4. Community and friends. The quality of the communities in which we participate has a strong influence upon how we feel. If we do not live and operate in communities and groups where there is a sense of trust and belonging then there is a raft of

evidence that shows the impact upon our ability to be happy.
5. Health. In studies people frequently cite health as an important contributor to happiness. While we may be able to adapt to many things that happen to us physically, they can take an emotional toll. When it comes to chronic pain and mental illness adaptation is more difficult and there should be a priority placed upon controlling suffering.[20]

Also Important:
6. Personal freedom. Happiness also depends upon the quality of the political, economic, legal and social systems in which we operate. There is some evidence that people living in stable and peaceful societies in which they have a voice and an ability to follow their interests (where it does not harm others), and in which institutions are accountable will be happier.[21]
7. Personal values. People's happiness depends on their "inner selves" and philosophies of life. "People are happier if they are able to appreciate what they have, whatever it is; if they do not always compare themselves with others; and if they school their own moods."[22] As Parker Palmer has put it, it is difficult to see how people can come to know others, or the world, if they do not know themselves. And, in turn, it is difficult to overcome "the pain of disconnection" if we do not attend to matters of the spirit.[23]

Therefore, the loss of community has detrimental effects both socially and individually. When our relationships decline and deep interactions are reduced, we have limited a powerful piece of the behavioral change process. We lack mentors who can model behaviors for us. We lack those who could share with the wisdom that comes from age and experience. We do not have people in place who can help us work through our emotions. We have limited resources to help edit our lives into the image of Christ.

Since the environments in which we grow up and the environments in which we live provide experiences that are engrained within us, we need to consider the environments and communities that we participate in. Changing behavior may require us to change communities thereby changing what influences us. Changing communities will influence our identity. I will share more on that later.

**Bringing it all Together**

Recently, I was on the social networking site Facebook. I was looking around to see which friends were in the chat area. I noticed that a high school friend, Kim Denson Cook, was online so I started a conversation with her. Kim makes handmade items, and I knew of a website where people could sell their handmade wares and I wanted to make sure she knew of it. In fact, I was hoping to see some items because I thought my wife or mother might like something from her collection.

During the course of that conversation, Kim asked me how my workouts were going. She hadn't seen me mention those recently and was just asking. Maya is the fitness coach for *My Fitness Coach* for the Wii, and in the afternoons, I would often tweet that I was about to spend time with Maya. My twitter account is connected to my Facebook account and so my tweets would show up on Facebook. Kim noticed that I had not made those posts in a while and called me on it! The truth, and what Kim didn't know, was that life got busy for about six weeks and I was in and out of the house making it difficult to engage in my regular exercise routine.

Yet, her question really affected me. Kim and I did not hang out much. We met during my junior and senior years of high school. I videotaped the basketball games and rode on the bus with the basketball team to away games. Kim was a cheerleader and a year younger than I was. Because the cheerleaders went to the games, she rode on those same buses. She was (and still is) a great person with a great smile. However, we did not really run in the same circles. Though I loved and played sports, I was known as the brainy, nerd type (some say I still am) who was involved in everything and knew everybody but really hung out with only a close set of friends. We mostly played full-contact badminton (it's a real sport where I came from), did our own theme interpretations of literary masterpieces, and played *Dungeons and Dragons*. (Ironically, I was always the cleric!) Kim, on the other hand, was a popular cheerleader on a nationally ranked squad. Those two groups do not tend to hang out together.

Yet, that simple question made a huge impression on me. It also illustrates the importance of community and relationships in changing behavior. Kim was concerned and interested enough in me to not only ask me that question, but to cheer me on when I started working out again. In fact, I often think of her asking that question every afternoon around 3:00, which is when I usually tweeted workouts. Once, after posting on twitter that I had exercised, Kim responded with "Go David, Go David, Go David!"

Kim's actions illustrate the whole rewiring process. I had

engaged in a countering technique, exercise, to deal with some of my own unhealthy behaviors. In noticing that I had not announced my exercising for a few weeks, Kim effectively became an editor in my life. By challenging me about the broken exercise pattern, she confronted me in a healthy way. When I re-engaged exercising, Kim provided me with a reward, cheering me on, which reinforced the new behavior.

This is the power of communities such as small groups, communities of Faith, or AA groups. It provides a place where people can journey together. The community challenges those on the journey together, creating a support structure for encouragement, and reward. It also provides another function. The practices embedded in the community shape the identities of those who participate. Engagement in the community socializes the behaviors of those in the community. Behaviors adapt, matching the embedded practices of the community. New experiences within the community create new emotions that form new ways of thinking. New habits are also formed. The person is re-formed through the community, resulting in a new identity.

A life holy rewired, therefore, has us finding our identity in a Christ-shaped community whose practices help shape us into a reflection of the image of Christ.

# BEING YOU

The movie *Freedom Writers* is based on the true story of Erin Gruwell. In the movie, Erin is a first-year teacher assigned to a group of students that the school administration had written off as failures. She is told that the majority of the students will drop out of school and live as street kids, gang members and thugs. Erin, played in the movie by Hilary Swank, does not accept the assertion of the school leaders. Through a variety of creative approaches, she helps the students see a larger picture of the world and helps them envision a new identity. As the students grasp a different identity, their behavior begins to change. They stay in school, their grades improve, and many actually graduate.[1]

How people react is a reflection of who they understand themselves to be. Therefore, in order for people to fully rewire their lives, there has to be a change in who they understand themselves to be.[2] When that happens, they are then able to understand their identity. The problem is that few people understand who and whose they are.

## Imago Dei

God provides an infinite, limitless perspective that expresses the infinite love of the infinite Creator to his finite, created beings. As the creator, he knows everything. He defines love because He is love. He defines life because He is life. As the one in whom everything fits and is held together, God is able to provide a perspective that the created cannot hold. This point of reference provides an absolute measure, a true north, not based on a limited understanding or cultural norms. It is safe to say, then, that a finite person's true identity is only found in the context of a relationship with the infinite God, His people, and with the scriptures.[3]

A biblical understanding of identity must begin in understanding how humankind was created. Genesis 1:26-27 provides that answer. God created humans in His own image to be a reflection of himself. Humanity was also created for relationships with both God and others. Genesis 2 tells us that Adam longed for someone like himself. God created Eve so that Adam could have community. In Genesis 2, we find this community present as God, Adam and Eve walked and talked in the garden together. In this relationship, both God and humanity were acting out of their character and identity.

However, when Adam and Eve chose to disobey God, the image of God in humankind was cracked and the relationship was broken, introducing sin to the human race.[4] As a result, humanity has a distorted identity inherited from its ancestor Adam.[5] Having a broken identity that is self-oriented rather than oriented towards Christ, humanity both collectively and individually creates a destructive and broken environment that perpetuates humankind's broken and perverted identity.

This perverted identity, because of this inherited identity, continues to be expressed in all of humankind. In other words, because of the Fall, humanity does not truly know who it is, and before any behavior can change in the deepest levels of life, a person has to replace this rebellious and prideful identity. As long as that identity of the first Adam remains in control, a person may change his or her behaviors in the short term, but long-term, holistic change will be evasive.

Yet, changing one behavior does not make a person whole. In fact, changing one behavior can result in other negative behaviors because behaviors are often masked by other symptoms.[6] For instance, addictive behaviors often result from a need to control or be comforted. A person may be able to overcome an addiction to food born from a sense of control or need for comfort, yet because he has not addressed those issues that caused the addiction, he fills the void with other addictive behaviors such as alcohol or shopping. Researchers call this addiction transfer.[7] Negative behavior is the symptom of deeper issues, just as a fever is a sign of infection. Controlling the fever is important, but controlling it alone is insufficient. Likewise, controlling negative behavior, while important, is just as insufficient.[8]

The Bible teaches that wholeness does not come primarily from changing our behavior but from being "in Christ". Only then can the journey towards wholeness begin.

God has declared that Christ-followers are "in Christ."[9] By gaining a clear view of what it means to be "in Christ," a person can have a glimpse inside the core of life's meaning and mystery.[10] Being in Christ "is not only the fundamental fact of the individual Christian's existence, it is the whole new reality."[11]

The expressions "in Christ," "in the beloved," "in him," or similar phrases are used over one hundred times in Scripture to refer to Christ-followers. In one sense, "in Christ" indicates a place.[12] A person "in Christ" is in a specific locale, and that locale is Jesus Christ. It is a positional transition. We are moved into a relationship with Christ.

It also indicates an ontological change, or a change relating to essence or the nature of our being.[13] By being "in Christ," the Christ-follower has been given a new footing for his or her existence.[14] The person has been recreated in, and into Christ. In Christ, "we have been given a share in the status enjoyed by Jesus Christ…We are sons of God *in* the Son of God. And this means nothing less than that we are infused with the divinized human life of Christ himself."[15] However, this does not mean that people become "little gods". It also does not mean that people are promoted to divinity after death. "Theosis means that humans become *like* God."[16] Michael Gorman notes that particularly in the writings of Paul, theosis "is the transformative participation in the kenotic, cruciform character of God through Spirit-enabled conformity to the incarnate, crucified, and resurrected/glorified Christ."[17] Gorman goes on to say that for Paul,

> *theosis takes place in the person and especially the community that is in Christ and within whom/within which Christ resides, as his Spirit molds and shapes the individual and community into the cruciform image of Christ. But this process of transformation takes some human cooperation, including especially contemplation of the exalted crucified One (2 Cor 3:18). For Paul, this is not merely a form of ancient, perhaps vacuous, mysticism, but a sustained reflection on, and identification with, the narrative pattern of Christ crucified and of its paradoxical power to bring life out of death (2 Cor 4:7-12), all enabled by God himself at work in the individual and community (Phil 2:12-13).*[18]

Becoming "in Christ," or the process of theosis, is the process whereby we participate with God as He transforms us into the image of Christ. In doing so we become fully human, for Christ was the human we were designed to be in Genesis 1:26-27. Christ's kenotic expression – his self-emptying, self-sacrifice on the cross – not only revealed what God was like but also what humans ought to be like.[19]

As a result, the image of Christ is the greatest thirst of our being. It is the most profound yearning of a person's life, though in our brokenness, we fill it with all kinds of inadequate substitutes. The image of Christ is that which brings "cleansing, healing, restoration, renewal, transformation, and wholeness into the unclean, diseased, broken, imprisoned, dead incompleteness of our lives. It brings compassion in place of indifference, forgiveness in place of resentment, kindness in place of coldness, openness in place of protective defensiveness or manipulation, a life lived for God and not self."[20]

This is the work of the Spirit in our lives. Repeatedly, the New Testament tells us that the work of the Spirit is to grow us toward Christlikeness. For instance, Paul says in 2 Corinthians 3:18, *"So all of us who have had that veil removed can see and reflect the glory of the Lord. And the Lord—who is the Spirit—makes us more and more like him as we are changed into his glorious image."* (NLT) This process will take place in those areas where we are not yet conformed into that image. We will be confronted in some fashion with that reality. Through some channel, such as the scriptures, worship, teaching, a friend, or some other event, the Spirit of God will probe an area where we are not conformed to the image of Christ. That part of us that is not yet conformed into Christ's image is not simply a thing to us; it is an essential part of who we are. It is these areas of our life that

Jesus points to when he calls us to take up our cross.

Taking up our cross is something that every one who follows Jesus must deal with.[21] Taking up our cross is not some difficult person we have to deal with day after day. It is not an employer or employee we cannot get along with. It is not someone whose actions annoy us whenever we see him or her. Nor is it the difficulties of life. Robert Mulholland states that our cross "is the point of our unlikeness to the image of Christ, where we must die to self in order to be raised by God into wholeness of life in the image of Christ *right there at that point.*"[22]

Additionally, whenever there is something in our life that does not conform to the image of Christ, there is a place

> *where we are incapable of being all that God wants us to be with others; there is a place where our life with others is hindered and limited and restricted in its effectiveness and in its fullness; there is a place where our life will tend to become disruptive and even destructive to others. We can never be all that God wants to be with others as long as that point of unlikeness to the image of Christ exists within us.*[23]

Being formed into the image of Christ reduces those points of unlikeness that create tension and conflict with others. It also continues us on a journey towards wholeness. — lifelong

When we are confronted by that unlikeness, we have to come to the point of saying "Yes" to God at each of those points. We must give God permission to do the work God wants to do with us. Transformation is not forced upon us; it is a choice we make. Though God will continue to press those points, knocking at the door of our lives, he will not force open the doors. The writer George MacDonald writes, "He watches to see the door move from within."[24]

If we are being formed into the *imago Christi*, the image of Christ, we have to engage in surrender. Being formed or being conformed goes against our very nature. As broken *eikons*, we are attempting to be God ourselves. As a result, we have attempted to take over control of our lives. We have great problems sitting still and letting God act in His time.

Mulholland says that we are an "objectivizing, informational-functional culture."[25] "An objectivizing culture," he states, "is one that views the world primarily as an object 'out there' to be grasped and controlled for our own purposes. We are the subjects whose role in life is to appropriate the objects in our world and use them to impose our will upon the world."[26] The Quaker, Parker Palmer, notes something similar:

> *We are well-educated people who have been schooled in a way of knowing that treats the world as an object to be dissected and manipulated, a way of knowing that gives us power over the world... [We] have used [our] knowledge to rearrange the world to satisfy [our] drive for power, distorting and deranging life rather than loving it for the gift it is.*[27]

Therefore, being conformed goes "totally against the ingrained objectification perspective of our culture. Graspers powerfully resist being grasped by God. Manipulators strongly reject being shaped by God. Controllers are inherently incapable of yielding control to God. Spiritual formation is the great reversal: from being the subject who controls all other things to being a person who is shaped by the presence, purpose and power of God in all things."[28]

We are also an informational-functional culture, according to Mulholland. In this, we "seek to possess information, whether in the form of knowledge or in the form of techniques, in order that we might function more effectively to bring about the results we desire in the circumstances of our lives. We seek to be totally and completely in control of that process."[29] Yet wholeness is not "our setting out (by gathering information and applying it correctly) to find God (as an object 'out there' to be grasped and controlled by us). It is a journey of learning to yield ourselves to God and discovering where God will take us."[30]

A deeper dimension of this control is at work here, however. We tend to see control as essential to our being, meaning, value and purpose. We live as though our doing determines our being.[31] That living influences our views on wholeness and behavior. We have a tendency to believe that if only we *do* the right things we will *be* the right kind of Christian. We think our doing will bring about our being. We need to get the order straight. Our *doing* flows out of our *being*.

The journey towards wholeness, then, is a great reversal. It moves us from "acting to bring about the desired results in our lives to being acted upon by God and responding in ways that allow God to bring about God's purposes."[32] It involves losing ourselves, surrendering the ingrained informational-functional orientation that governs not only our lives but also the lifestyle of our culture. It means that we relinquish our self-generated expectations. This involves restoring our being and doing to their proper relationship.

Identity into the *imago Christi* is not only God through the Holy Spirit acting on us, it is God acting on us in the context of a community. Because God is relational and social, we are wired to be relational and social. Therefore, our identity has a socially constructed element.

113

## The Social Context of Biblical Identity

There is a social aspect to all of humanity as stated in the early creation narrative, "Then the LORD God said, 'It is not good that the man should be alone; I will make him a helper fit for him.'"[33] The creation of the female alongside the male began a process whereby families, communities and societies were created. As part of being created in the image of God, humanity reflects the social nature of God, made for relationships with both God and others.[34] Community cannot be an option for it is necessary to being what humanity was created to be.[35]

In the Old Testament, the Jews organized their lives around the Temple and its festivals, as well as tribes and families. The desert tabernacle was the forerunner to the Temple, which became an essential part of the government and religious life of the people of Israel.[36] Though no one knows how or why it came into being, the synagogue, defined by tradition rather than biblical statute, arose.[37] It had a three-fold purpose: (1) to be a place of assembly for the public discussion and celebration of meals; (2) a place of study; and (3) a place of prayer. It was a place where the Torah was read and studied.[38]

After the Jerusalem temple was destroyed, the synagogue and the home took over many of its functions. The holidays that were originally practiced in the temple were now celebrated within the synagogue or the home.[39] The ritual of the synagogue is an adaptation of the ritual of the temple. However, almost every Jewish holiday and ritual had a focus in the home with only a secondary focus at the synagogue.[40] Additionally, instructing children occurred within the context of the family.[41] Through festivals and meals, as well as through family instruction, Jewish identity developed through socialization and enculturation primarily in the purview of the family.[42]

In the New Testament, Jesus began to redefine the Jewish community experience. In the calling of the twelve disciples, Jesus called people out of the biological and racial family context of community into a new community experience. Referring to the statements of Jesus in Matthew 10:37 and Luke 14:26, Gerhard Lohfink states:

> *Thus Jesus required of his disciples a determined turning away from their own families – this is what is meant by hate. Common life with Jesus took the place of family and all previous ties. This common life meant more than merely being with a teacher, listening to him and observing him, in order to learn the Torah from his statements and his manner of life. The disciple's community of life with Jesus was a community of destiny. It went so far that the disciples had to be prepared to suffer what Jesus suffered – if necessary, even persecution or execution.*[43]

Jesus would even go so far as to restate whom his own family was, though he did not disown his biological family. In Mark 3:35, Jesus states, "Whoever does the will of God, he is my brother and sister and mother." He rejected pleas by his biological family to come back with him, instead choosing to be part of his new family organized around the Kingdom of God. To quote David Garland, in his commentary on Mark,

> *Jesus' response to the visit from his family would have been a shocker because it runs counter to the received wisdom of the age. The family was the basis of social and economic*

*life and the source of one's identity. In the first-century Mediterranean world, an individual's identity was basically that of a member of a group. The genealogies and laws relating to family life in the Scriptures show the importance of membership in a family or clan (and village). In the Old Testament, "life" is used almost interchangeably with "family". One's family was one's life, and to reject family or to be cast out of a family was to lose one's life.*

*But Jesus affirms that life under God is not defined by relationships in a biological family…One's ultimate devotion is owed to God, who is head of a new divine family, and becoming a member of this family is open to all persons regardless of race, class, or gender. The only requirement is that they share Jesus' commitment to God.*[44]

Jesus thus transforms spiritual community formed from a national, familial, and racial scope to a community formed around the presence of God. Ironically, Jewish community originally centered around the presence of God, as typified in temple life and ritual.[45]

This transformation by Jesus led to the emphasis in Pauline literature that places community in the context of a loving family. Jesus stands behind Paul's usage in this manner. In the Spirit of Christ, the early Christian communities strived to become familial and familiar settings where love could be learned.[46] Christians are to see themselves as members of a divine family.[47] Referencing Garland's thoughts above, then by being part of a divine family one finds their identity and life within the family of God, not within themselves because the "gospel is not a purely personal matter. It has a social dimension. It is a communal affair."[48]

*Being You*

## Rebirth

An elder religious leader wanted to have a discussion with the up and coming teacher, so he scheduled a meeting for the coming evening. The questioning began and the followers of these two religious teachers were fully engaged in the discussion. It was then that the younger challenged his elder with a confounding statement, "You must be born again."

The elder leader replied:

> *"How can anyone," said Nicodemus, "be born who has already been born and grown up? You can't re-enter your mother's womb and be born again. What are you saying with this 'born-from-above' talk?"*
>
> *Jesus said, "You're not listening. Let me say it again. Unless a person submits to this original creation—the 'wind-hovering-over-the-water' creation, the invisible moving the visible, a baptism into a new life—it's not possible to enter God's kingdom. When you look at a baby, it's just that: a body you can look at and touch. But the person who takes shape within is formed by something you can't see and touch—the Spirit—and becomes a living spirit.* (John 3:4-6, *The Message*)

John Mark, the writer of the book of Mark, tells the story of an encounter where Jesus rebukes his disciples for keeping children from touching Jesus. "The people brought children to Jesus, hoping he might touch them. The disciples shooed them off. But Jesus was irate and let them know it: "Don't push these children away. Don't ever get between them and me. These children are at the very center of life in the kingdom. Mark this: Unless you accept God's kingdom in the simplicity of a child, you'll never get in." Then, gathering the children up in his arms, he laid his hands of blessing on them." (Mark 10:13-15, *The Message*)

The disciples, in one of their more selfish moments, were wondering who might be the highest rank in Jesus' kingdom. Jesus' response?

> *For an answer Jesus called over a child, whom he stood in the middle of the room, and said, "I'm telling you, once and for all, that unless you return to square one and start over like children, you're not even going to get a look at the kingdom, let alone get in. Whoever becomes simple and elemental again, like this child, will rank high in God's kingdom. What's more, when you receive the childlike on my account, it's the same as receiving me. (*Matthew 18:2-5, *The Message*)

Paul said "Now we look inside, and what we see is that anyone united with the Messiah gets a fresh start, is created new. The old life is gone; a new life burgeons!"[49]

Union with Jesus places us on a journey to wholeness. It is a journey that requires a new identity.

Jesus talked of the process as becoming a little child. He used these phrases to remind the disciples that entering into the kingdom requires a new birth, becoming young, having a faith that is child-like in its simplicity and devoted trust. It is a new way of living.

We noted earlier that our identity is formed by our relationships, our experiences, our thinking about ourselves, and the emotions that are formed by this connected triad. Our new identity is also shaped in the same manner. Getting there, however, is the process of becoming like a little child. It is the process of unlearning. It is a process of rebirth.

We have an identity built up on years of both painful and positive experiences. We have experienced great relational loss, as in the loss of a close family member or friend to death. We have had relationships go sour. We also have had the joy of family experiences, great vacations and overcoming great challenges. Through these experiences, we have learned to act a certain way and to think a certain way and to feel a certain way.

The process of rebirth, then, is a process of "unlearning". The Holy Spirit helps us unlearn old ways of thinking and old ways of acting. We unlearn the emotions that resulted from those painful experiences. We unlearn old habits that have become so comfortable and familiar to us. We unlearn an old way of living that created anxiety, worry, and craving. Rebirth is the difficult process of unlearning, a process focused on forming us into the image of Christ. In fact, it is harder for most people to unlearn than to learn.

Rebirth is not only unlearning, but of new learning. It is a journey where the Spirit gives us new experiences, new relationships and a new focus. In doing that, our new identity is in the process of being re-formed into the image of Christ. That new identity allows us to see ourselves as God sees us and to act the way we were created to act. We are his children. We are his sons and daughters. And he gave everything for us!

Through this re-birthing process, we not only are God's child, positionally, but we become his child relationally. Rebirthing puts in the place of being God's child while at the same time puts on a journey of becoming God's child. The adoption process is like that. In adoption, a child becomes a son or daughter positionally, through the legal process. In many cases, it takes time, however, for that boy or girl to feel like they are a son or daughter relationally.

Through that process of unlearning and new learning, there comes a moment where we realize not with our mind but with our heart that we are God's son or daughter. We are no longer a son or daughter positionally, but relationally. We are able to trust fully. We are able to not worry about anything. Why? Because we know that the God of the entire universe will take care of us no matter the scenario, even the scenario of death. We are able to think and act out of our new identity. This is important because we "cannot consistently behave in ways that are different from what we believe about ourselves."[50] If we know experientially and relationally that we are God's son or daughter, we can now act out of that identity.

We are now, however, living in an "in between" period. The wholeness that we long for is not attainable fully in this life. It can only happen when we are in full and total presence of the one who created us. It can only happen when we are able to enter the re-created garden where our relationship with God is not clouded by the effects of sin and evil. All of us long for that "Unclouded Day", as expressed in the song by Willie Nelson:

> *They tell me of a home where my friends have gone*
> *And they tell me of that land far away*
> *Where the tree of life in eternal bloom*
> *Sheds its fragrance through the unclouded day*
>
> *They tell me of the King in His beauty there*
> *And they tell me that mine eyes shall behold*
> *Where He sits on a throne that is whiter than snow*
> *In the city that is made of gold*

*Being You*

*They tell me that He smiles on His children there
And His smile drives their sorrows away
And they tell me that no tears ever come again
In that lovely land of unclouded day*

*O the land of cloudless days
O the land of an unclouded sky
O They tell me of a home where no storm clouds rise
O They tell me of an unclouded day*

So while the journey is not completely attainable in this life, it is a journey that shapes us increasingly into the image of Christ, into a life of peace and contentment that allows us to live as *eikons* of God in a broken world.

## REWIRING TAKES TIME

    Working as a programmer and manager in the IT industry meant I also did my share of grunt work. I have had to pull many ethernet cables, install new ethernet cabling in buildings, and move servers and computers from one building to another. In one company, we moved a set of servers that we had configured in our offices in Tampa to a datacenter in Atlanta. We labeled and documented everything before we left Tampa. When we got to the datacenter in Atlanta, we unpacked everything and meticulously went about the process of making sure the servers were stacked in the same configuration as they were in our offices and that the cabling was the same in the switches. This took a lot of time and energy. The outcome, however, was that it was easy for everyone in the organization to be able to walk into that datacenter and know where everything went and the function of each server. In that rack of servers and cabling, a discernable order and meaning existed, allowing them to function together.

    I have also walked into a datacenter to see a rack of computers in utter chaos. Trying to figure out which server performed a specific function was a nightmare. In addition, trying to track down a cabling issue meant that a co-worker and I had to deconstruct the entire stack to determine the problem. It took hours to determine what everything did, why things were not working, and then put it all back together.

Many of our lives are a jumbled mess of bad habits and painful emotions. It is hard to identify what is wrong with our lives or even who we are or what meaning our life has. Too often, we give up trying to change behavior or find wholeness. Maybe you feel like it is easier to live in the brokenness that is comfortable for us than to strain and struggle for a new way of life.

**God does not want you to stay there!**

The Gospel invites you on a journey towards wholeness. It is not, however, a short ride to the friend across town. It is a cross-country trip full of stops and starts, detours and mistakes. The Gospel is a journey that takes us where we do not think we want to go. But in taking us there, it allows us to experience beauty and truth and love we never otherwise would experience.

The Chinese philosopher Lao-tzu said, "A journey of a thousand miles begins with a single step." With apologies to Mr. tzu, the journey of a thousand miles is really our life's journey, and it begins earlier than the first step. The journey begins with the decision to let the one who created you re-form you into his image so that you reflect God back to himself and also reflect God out to a broken world.

# NOTES

## **The Problem**

¹ Dietrich Bonhoeffer, John W. De Gruchy, and Douglas S. Bax, *Creation and Fall: A Theological Exposition of Genesis 1-3* (Minneapolis: Fortress Press, 1997), 84.

² Ibid., 72.

³ Tatha Wiley, *Original Sin: Origins, Developments, Contemporary Meanings* (New York: Paulist Press, 2002). 35.

⁴ Stanley Grenz, *The Social God and the Relational Self: A Trinitarian Theology of the Imago Dei.* (Louisville, KY.: Westminster John Knox Press, 2001), 204.

⁵ Charles Sherlock, *The Doctrine of Humanity* (Downers Grove, IL: InterVarsity Press, 1996). 42.

⁶ Ibid.

⁷ Blaise Pascal and A. J. Krailsheimer, *Pensées*, Rev. ed., Penguin Classics (London New York: Penguin Books; Penguin Books USA, 1995), 45.

⁸ Ron Martoia, Static: Tune out the "Christian Noise" and Experience the Real Message of Jesus (Carol Stream, Ill.: Tyndale House Publishers, 2007). 170.

⁹ Martoia, 160.

¹⁰ Ibid.

¹¹ Richard Rohr, Andreas Ebert, and Peter Heinegg, *The Enneagram: A Christian Perspective* (New York: Crossroad Pub., 2001), 34.

¹² Martoia, 170.

¹³ Bonhoeffer, 113. See also Ron Martoia, *Static: Tune out the "Christian Noise" and Experience the Real Message of Jesus* (Carol Stream, Ill.: Tyndale House Publishers, 2007). 118.

¹⁴ Wiley, 5.

¹⁵ Colin Brown and David Townsley, *The New International Dictionary of New Testament Theology*, 4 vols. (Grand Rapids, Mich.: Regency Reference Library, 1986)., 2:181.

¹⁶ Ibid.

¹⁷ Ibid.

¹⁸ Ibid.

¹⁹ Brown and Townsley, 2:182.

²⁰ Ibid.

## Notes

[21] Ibid.

[22] Anthony Hoekema, *Created in God's Image* (Grand Rapids: William B. Eerdmans Publishing, 1986), 104.

[23] Leslie S. Greenberg and Sandra C. Paivio, *Working with Emotions in Psychotherapy*, Practicing Professional (New York: Guilford Press, 1997), 14.

[24] Daniel Goleman, *Emotional Intelligence* (New York: Bantam Books, 1995), 9, 14.

[25] Greenberg and Paivio, 15-17.

[26] See any number of Gospel presentations such as "The Roman's Road," "Evangelism Explosion" and "Continuous Witness Training."

[27] Martoia, 200.

[28] Ibid., 221

[29] Ibid., 36.

[30] Ibid., 61-62.

[31] Ibid., 62.

[32] Sherlock, 50.

[33] Bonhoffer, in *Creation and Fall* states, "The prohibition [against the tree of the knowledge of good and evil] means nothing other than this: Adam, you are who you are because of

me, your Creator; so now be what you are. (85)" From this, I deduce that finding our identity places us back into the Garden, though a metaphorical garden.

[34] This is a term I am deriving from an integration of "in Christ" and Murray Bowen's concept of self-differentiation. See Michael E. Kerr and Murray Bowen, *Family Evaluation: The Role of the Family as an Emotional Unit That Governs Individual Behavior and Development*, (New York: W. W. Norton & Company, 1988), 68.

[35] Peter Scazzero, *Emotionally Healthy Spirituality: Unleash the Power of Authentic Life in Christ*. (Nashville: Thomas Nelson, 2006), 24-25.

[36] Joseph E. LeDoux, *The Emotional Brain: The Mysterious Underpinnings of Emotional Life*. (New York: Simon & Schuster, 1996), 180.

[37] Ibid.

[38] Ibid., 181.

[39] Greenberg and Paivio, 99.

[40] Ibid.

[41] Leslie S. Greenberg and Jeremy D. Safran, *Emotion in Psychotherapy: Affect, Cognition, and the Process of Change* (New York: Guilford Press, 1987), 188.

[42] I John 2:6 gives us insight into this. The one who is in Christ

obeys His word and commandments. This really is an expression of relationship and wholeness. In doing so, we live as Jesus lived, having a mature love.

## **Change is Hard**

[1] Alan Deutschman, *Change or Die*. http://www.fastcompany.com/magazine/94/open_change-or-die.html (accessed February 20, 2009)

[2] Ibid.

[3] Ibid.

[4] Ibid.

[5] Richard J. Foster, *Celebration of Discipline: The Path to Spiritual Growth* (New York: HarperCollins, 1988), 5.

[6] Ibid.

[7] Ibid., 6.

[8] Donald S. Whitney, *Spiritual Disciplines for the Christian Life* (Colorado Springs: NavPress, 1991), 15.

[9] Foster, 3.

[10] Ibid., 6.

[11] Ibid., 4.

[12] Edwin H. Friedman, *A Failure of Nerve: Leadership in the Age of*

the *Quick Fix* (New York: Seabury Books, 2007), 81.

[13] Foster, 8.

[14] Keith S. Ditman and others, "A Controlled Experiment on the Use of Court Probation for Drunk Arrests," *American Journal of Psychiatry* 124, no. 2 (1967).

[15] D. C. Walsh and others, "A Randomized Trial of Treatment Options for Alcohol-Abusing Workers," *New England Journal of Medicine* 325, no. 11 (1991).

[16] Ibid.

[17] Ibid.

[18] Ibid.

[19] Ferri MMF, Amato L, Davoli M. Alcoholics Anonymous and other 12-Step Programmes for Alcohol Dependence. *Cochrane Database of Systematic Reviews 2006*, Issue 3. Art. No.: CD005032

[20] Mauro Barbosa Terra and others, "Do Alcoholics Anonymous Groups Really Work? Factors of Adherence in a Brazilian Sample of Hospitalized Alcohol Dependents," *American Journal on Addictions* 17, no. 1 (2008).

[21] G. Atkins Randolph and E. Hawdon James, "Religiosity and Participation in Mutual-Aid Support Groups for Addiction," *Journal of Substance Abuse Treatment* 33, no. 3 (2007).

[22] Ibid.

[23] Ibid.

[24] "How Effective Is Alcoholics Anonymous?" *Harvard Mental Health Letter* 20, no. 6 (2003).

[25] Ibid.

[26] *The Effectiveness of and Need for Professional Counseling Services* (American Counseling Association, 2008).

[27] Ibid.

[28] Roger Baker and others, "A Naturalistic Longitudinal Evaluation of Counseling in Primary Care," *Counseling Psychology Quarterly* 15, no. 4 (2002).

[29] Ibid.

[30] Ibid.

[31] Ibid.

[32] Douglas L. Polcin, "Professional Counseling Versus Specialized Programs for Alcohol and Drug Abuse Treatment," *Journal of Addictions & Offender Counseling* 21, no. October (2000).

[33] Ibid.

[34] Alan Deutschman, *Change or Die.* http://www.fastcompany.com/magazine/94/open_change-or-die.html (accessed February 20, 2009)

35 Ibid.

## **Who you have Become**

1 Norman Doidge, *The Brain That Changes Itself: Stories of Personal Triumph from the Frontiers of Brain Science* (New York: Viking, 2007), xiii-xv.

2 Begley, 102.

3 Christopher D. Frith, *Making up the Mind: How the Brain Creates Our Mental World* (Malden, MA: Blackwell Pub., 2007), 128.

4 Peter Scazzero, *The Emotionally Healthy Church.* (Grand Rapids: Zondervan Publishing, 2003), 95.

5 1 Corinthians 15:30-34

6 Romans 9:10-12.

7 Rick H. Hoyle, Selfhood: Identity, Esteem, Regulation, Social Psychology Series (Boulder, Colo.: Westview, 1999), 31.

8 Ibid., 32.

9 Ibid., 36.

10 Ibid.

11 Ibid.

12 Ibid.

13 Dianne M. Tice, "Self-Concept Change and Self-

Presentation: The Looking Glass Self Is Also a Magnifying Glass," *Journal of Personality and Social Psychology* 63, no. 3 Sep 1992 (1992).

## **Broken Emotions**

[1] Alan Deutschman, *Change or Die.* http://www.fastcompany.com/magazine/94/open_change-or-die.html (accessed February 20, 2009)

[2] Ibid.

[3] Beverley Fehr and James A. Russell, "Concept of Emotion Viewed from a Prototype Perspective," *Journal of Experimental Psychology - General* 113, no. 3 (1984), 464.

[4] Ibid.

[5] Paul Thomas Young, *Motivation of Behavior: The Fundamental Determinants of Human and Animal Activity* (New York, London: J. Wiley & Sons inc.; Chapman & Hall limited, 1936), 450.

[6] Ibid.

[7] William E. Lyons, *Emotion* (New York: Cambridge University Press, 1980), 60.

[8] Goleman, 6.

[9] Ibid.

[10] R.L. Koteskey, "Toward the Development of Christian Psychology- Emotion," *Journal of Psychology and Theology* 8, no. 4

(1980), 304-305.

[11] Goleman, 15.

[12] Ibid., 14.

[13] Ibid., 15.

[14] Ibid.

[15] LeDoux, 163.

[16] Goleman, 23.

[17] Ibid., 24.

[18] Ibid.

[19] Ibid., 24-25.

[20] Ibid., 25.

[21] Ibid., 26.

[22] Ibid.

[23] Ibid.

[24] Goleman, 14.

[25] Ann Marie Barry, *Visual Intelligence: Perception, Image, and Manipulation in Visual Communication* (Albany: State University of New York Press, 1997), 18.

## *Notes*

[26] Barry, 15.

[27] Ibid.

[28] LeDoux, 181.

[29] Ibid.

[30] Ibid.

[31] Ibid., 182.

[32] Ibid, 27.

[33] Greenberg and Paivio, 14.

[34] Ibid.

[35] Ibid.

[36] Ibid., 18.

[37] Ibid.

[38] LeDoux, 180.

[39] Ibid.

[40] LeDoux, 180-181.

[41] Ibid., 181.

[42] Ibid., 182.

[43] Ibid.

[44] Ibid., 200-203.

[45] Ibid., 203.

[46] Ibid.

[47] Eugene Winograd and Ulric Neisser, *Affect and Accuracy in Recall: Studies Of "Flashbulb" Memories*, Emory Symposia in Cognition; 4 (Cambridge ; New York, NY, USA: Cambridge University Press, 1992), 9-10.

[48] LeDoux, 211.

[49] Ibid.

[50] Angier, Natalie, Memory Quirks: The human brain processes different data in different ways (and a catchy tune doesn't hurt). http://www2.journalnow.com/content/2009/jul/07/memory-quirks-the-human-brain-processes-different-/living/, accessed July 8, 2009.

[51] Ibid.

[52] Chris Brewin, *Cognitive Foundations of Clinical Psychology* (London: Lawrence Erlbaum Associates, 1988), 42.

[53] Ibid., 43.

[54] Duke University. "Emotional Memories Function In Self-Reinforcing Loop." *ScienceDaily* 24 March 2005.

*Notes*

http://www.sciencedaily.com/releases/2005/03/050323130625.htm, accessed July 8, 2009.

**Wiring the Brain**

[1] Richard M. Restak, *The Naked Brain: How the Emerging Neurosociety Is Changing How We Live, Work, and Love*, 1st ed. (New York: Harmony Books, 2006), 22.

[2] Restak, 22.

[3] Ibid..

[4] Ibid., 24.

[5] Ibid.

[6] Ibid.

[7] Ibid.

[8] Ibid.

[9] Ibid.

[10] Ibid., 105.

[11] Ibid.

[12] Ibid.

[13] Ibid.

[14] Ibid.

[15] Ibid.

[16] Ibid., 106.

[17] David Tenenbaum, "'Home-Grown' Proteins Build Synaptic Strength," *HHMI Bulletin* 14, no. 4 (2001).

[18] Schwartz and Begley, 107.

[19] Sharon Begley, *Train Your Mind, Change Your Brain: How a New Science Reveals Our Extraordinary Potential to Transform Ourselves* (New York: Ballantine Books, 2007), 30.

[20] Ibid.

[21] LeDoux, 211.

[22] Begley, 30.

[23] Ibid., 6.

[24] Ibid.

[25] Read Montague, *Why Choose This Book? How We Make Decisions* (New York: Dutton, 2006), 15.

[26] Christian Casanova and Maurice Ptito, *Vision: From Neurons to Cognition, Progress in Brain Research; V. 134* (Amsterdam ; New York: Elsevier Science, 2001), 427.

[27] Ibid., 437.

[28] Begley, 114-115.

[29] Doidge, 211.

[30] Begley, 115

[31] Begley, 115-116.

[32] Montague, xvi

[33] Ibid.

[34] Louis J. Cozolino, *The Neuroscience of Psychotherapy: Building and Rebuilding the Human Brain*, Norton Series on Interpersonal Neurobiology (New York: Norton, 2002), 22.

[35] Ibid.

[36] Ibid., 23.

[37] Ibid., 131.

[38] Ibid., 133-134.

[39] Doidge, 165.

[40] Ibid.

[41] Ibid.

[42] Ibid.

[43] Ibid., 165-167.

[44] Ibid., 169.

⁴⁵ Ibid.

⁴⁶ Adel K. Afifi and Ronald A. Bergman, *Functional Neuroanatomy: Text and Atlas*, 2nd ed. (New York: Lange Medical Books/McGraw-Hill, 2005), 31.

⁴⁷ Doige, 169-170.

⁴⁸ Ibid., 170.

⁴⁹ Ibid., 171.

⁵⁰ Ibid., 172.

⁵¹ Ibid., 174.

⁵² Ibid.

⁵³ Ibid.

⁵⁴ Ibid.

⁵⁵ Begley, 141.

⁵⁶ Ibid.

⁵⁷ Guang Yue Aand Kelly J. Cole, "Strength Increases from the Motor Program: Comparison of Training with Maximal Voluntary and Imagined Muscle Contractions," *Journal of Neurophysiology* 67, no. 5 (1992).

⁵⁸ Doidge, 204.

*Notes*

## The Change Process

[1] Daniel Goleman, Richard E. Boyatzis, and Annie McKee, *Primal Leadership: Realizing the Power of Emotional Intelligence* (Boston, Mass.: Harvard Business School Press, 2002), 33.

[2] Bruce Wilson, *Primal Leadership and the Role of Listening in Emotional Intelligence, Part I* http://www.businesslistening.com/primal-leadership.php (accessed December 15 2008).

[3] Richard E. Boyatzis and Annie McKee, *Resonant Leadership: Renewing Yourself and Connecting with Others through Mindfulness, Hope, and Compassion* (Boston: Harvard Business School Press, 2005), 4.

[4] Ibid., 5.

[5] Ibid., 88.

## The Disciplines and Community

[1] Mulholland, 102.

[2] Ibid., 103.

[3] Ibid., 76.

[4] Ibid., 105.

[5] Ibid.

[6] Henri Nouwen, "Letting Go of All Things," *Soujourners,* May

1979, 6, quoted in Mulholland, 106.

[7] Ibid.

[8] Mulholland, 106.

[9] Ibid., 107.

[10] Ibid., 108.

[11] Ibid.

[12] Ibid., 110-111.

[13] Ibid., 111.

[14] Ibid., 112.

[15] Ibid., 114-115.

[16] 2 Timothy 3:16, NLT.

[17] Psalm 15:5, *The Message*.

## **Emotional Healing**

[1] Walter Bruegemann, *Isaiah 40-66*. (Louisville, KY: Westminster John Knox Press, 1998), 131.

[2] Leslie S. Greenberg and Sandra C. Paivio, *Working with Emotions in Psychotherapy*, Practicing Professional (New York: Guilford Press, 1997), 99.

[3] Ibid.

[4] Ibid.

[5] Boyatzis and McKee, 74-75.

## **Rewiring the Brain**

[1] James O. Prochaska, John C. Norcross, and Carlo C. Diclemente, *Changing for Good*. (New York: HarperCollins, 1995), 176.

[2] Ibid.

[3] Ibid., 177.

[4] Ibid.

[5] Ibid., 178.

[6] Ibid.

[7] Ibid., 179.

[8] Ibid.

[9] Ibid., 180.

[10] Ibid., 183.

[11] Ibid.

[12] Ibid.

[13] Ibid.

[14] Ibid., 183-184.

[15] Ibid., 184.

[16] Ibid.

[17] Ibid.

[18] Ibid., 186.

## A Community of Editors

[1] Daniel Goleman, *Social Intelligence: The Revolutionary New Science of Human Relationships.* (New York: Bantam Book, 2006), 4.

[2] Ibid., 5.

[3] Ibid., 11.

[4] Ibid., 291.

[5] Ibid.

[6] Ibid.

[7] Ibid., 41.

[8] Ibid.

[9] Ibid., 42.

[10] Ibid., 43

[11] I Corinthians 15:33 NLT

[12] Janet Kornblum, "Study: 25% of Americans have no one to confide in", http://www.usatoday.com/news/nation/2006-06-22-friendship_x.htm, accessed February 25, 2010.

[13] Mark Easton, "Life in UK 'has become lonelier'", http://news.bbc.co.uk/2/hi/uk_news/7755641.stm, accessed February 25, 2010.

[14] Ibid.

[15] Ibid.

[16] "Social Capital", http://www.infed.org/biblio/social_capital.htm, accessed March 18, 2010.

[17] Richard Layard, *Happiness: Lessons from a New Science* (New York: Penguin Press, 2005), 63.

[18] Ibid., 67.

[19] Ibid., 64.

[20] Ibid., 69.

[21] Ibid., 69-70.

[22] Ibid., 71.

[23] "Happiness and education - theory, practice and possibility", http://www.infed.org/biblio/happiness_and_education.htm, accessed March 18, 2010.

## **Being You**

[1] Eric Geiger, *Identity: Who You Are in Christ* (Nashville, TN: B&H Publishing, 2008), 11.

[2] Dennis McCallum, *Walking in Victory: Experiencing the Power of Your Identity in Christ* (Columbus, OH: Xenos Publishing, 2002), 13.

[3] Bonhoeffer, 62.

[4] Sherlock, 42.

[5] Sherlock, 61-65.

[6] Overeating Replaced With Other Compulsive Behaviors. http://www.intelihealth.com/IH/ihtIH/WSIHW000/333/8014/510565.html (accessed November 24, 2008).

[7] Ibid.

[8] McCallum, 19-20.

[9] Colossians 1:3.

[10] Lewis B. Smedes, *Union with Christ: A Biblical View of the New Life in Jesus Christ*, 2nd. rev. ed. (Grand Rapids, Mich.: Eerdmans, 1983), 59.

[11] Ibid.

[12] Ibid., 60.

*Notes*

[13] Ontological. http://dictionary.reference.com/browse/ontological (accessed: November 26, 2008).

[14] Smedes, 61.

[15] Ibid., 61-62.

[16] Michael J. Gorman, *Inhabiting the Cruciform God: Kenosis, Justification, and Theosis in Paul's Narrative Soteriology*, (Grand Rapids, Mich.: William B. Eerdmans, 2009), 5.

[17] Ibid., 7.

[18] Ibid., 93.

[19] Timothy Savage, *Power through Weakness: Paul's understanding of the Christian Ministry in 2 Corinthians*, SMTSMS 86 (Cambridge: Cambridge University Press, 1996), 152.

[20] Robert Mulholland, Jr., *Invitation to a Journey*, (Downers Grove, IL: IVP, 1993), 34.

[21] Luke 9:23.

[22] Mulholland, 38.

[23] Ibid., 41.

[24] C. S. Lewis, ed., *George MacDonald: An Anthology*. (New York: Macmillan, 1978), 37-38.

[25] Mulholland, 26.

[26] Ibid.

[27] Parker Price, *To Know as We are Known*. (New York: Harper & Row, 1983), 2.

[28] Mulholland, 27.

[29] Ibid.

[30] Ibid., 32.

[31] Ibid., 27.

[32] Ibid., 30-31.

[33] Genesis 2:18.

[34] Grenz, 52.

[35] Julie Gorman, *Community That Is Christian*, 2nd ed. (Grand Rapids, Mich.: Baker Books, 2002), 29.

[36] Richard N. Longenecker, *Community Formation in the Early Church and in the Church Today* (Peabody, Mass.: Hendrickson Publishers, 2002), 21.

[37] Ibid., 25.

[38] Ibid.

[39] Ibid., 29.

[40] Ibid.

*Notes*

[41] Gorman, 100.

[42] Ibid.

[43] Gerhard Lohfink, *Jesus and Community: The Social Dimension of Christian Faith* (Philadelphia: Fortress Press, 1984), 33.

[44] David E. Garland, *Mark* (Grand Rapids, Mich.: Zondervan Pub. House, 1996), 131.

[45] Longenecker, 21.

[46] Robert J. Banks, *Paul's Idea of Community*, Rev. ed. (Peabody, Mass.: Hendrickson Publishers, 1994), 56.

[47] Ibid , 49.

[48] Ibid , 26.

[49] 2 Corinthians 5:17, *The Message*

[50] Geiger, 1.